POWER PHRASES!

PowerPhrases™

POWER PHRASES!

The Perfect Words to Say It Right and Get the Results You Want

Meryl Runion

Power Potentials Publishing

Power Potentials Publishing
P.O. Box 187
Cascade CO 80809

Library of Congress Control Number: 2001095779

Publisher's Cataloging-in-Publication
(Provided by Quality Books, Inc.)

Runion, Meryl.
Power Phrases! : the perfect words to say it right and get the results you want / Meryl Runion ; editor Kristin Porotsky. -- 1st ed.

p. cm.

ISBN: 0-9714437-2-6

Third Printing

1. Business communication. 2. Oral Communication.
I. Porotsky, Kristin. II. Title.

HF5718.R86 2001 658.4'52

QBI01-201211

Table of Contents

NOTE FROM THE EDITOR

It began as a normal editing project, and became a powerful learning experience. When Meryl Runion first told me about her book idea, I thought she was on to something. When she asked me to edit it, I had no idea that I would become indoctrinated into the PowerPhrases phenomenon. Now, everywhere I turn, I see the need for PowerPhrases. Everyone I see needs the communications tools contained in these pages. My family, my friends, my neighbors need them - and I do too. When reading Dr. Seuss to my son I even wanted to teach Power Phrases to Thidwick, the Big-Hearted Moose. I hope this book is as successful as it deserves to be, because I want to edit the sequels.

Kristin Porotsky

Editor
Another Pair of Eyes
Mother of Two

Disclaimer

This book is designed to provide communications information and guidance. The publisher and the author are not offering legal or other professional services. Every effort has been made to offer advice that is accurate, sound and useful. Results vary in different situations. The author and the publisher cannot be held liable or responsible for any damages caused or allegedly caused directly or indirectly by the information in this book.

If you do not wish to be bound by the above, you may return this book to the publisher for a full refund.

Acknowledgements

I want to thank those who saw the vision that I saw when I decided to write this book. I believed that I had a valuable and useful idea from the very beginning, but the belief of others helped to keep me going.

Thanks to Bill Cowles of SkillPath Publications, whose belief in the idea kept me inspired.

I offer thanks to my editor, Kristin Porotsky. With two small children in tow, she took the time to carefully edit and often remembered to tell me that I was "awesome".

I take great inspiration from speaker and author Linda Larsen. Her insistence that this is "not just any book" and that I would have a "huge hit on my hands" gave me more courage than she will ever know.

The encouragement and advice of author Jay Conrad Levinson also provided much needed inspiration from a source that I deeply respect.

I must include my thanks to my dear friend Cindi Myers. After she started reading the manuscript she didn't stop. Her enthusiasm was an inspiration as well.

And of course, I want to thank my family, who allowed me to be married to my book for close to a year.

PREFACE

PowerPhrases™ are Born

One fall day in 1986 I was taking a CPR class for my work. On break I stopped by a grocery store. In the parking lot was a man lying unconscious. He had a circle of people standing around him, all doing nothing. "Oh no!" I thought, "Has he had a heart attack? Could it be that he needs CPR? I'm half trained…"

I had a habit of deferring to the authority of others. There was a man in the circle who stood there looking so in charge! I said in a soft little voice, "Maybe he needs CPR!" The response was as if I had not spoken at all. Rather than repeating myself or simply taking decisive action, I closed my mouth and stood watching with the others. I prayed that the ambulance would come in time. I never found out if that man lived or if he died.

When the ambulance did come and I went back to class, I was sick at heart. I thought about the people who loved him and I imagined how they would feel if they knew that someone who might have been able to help stood there watching instead. I did some serious soul searching.

While that was not the first time my lack of assertiveness limited me, it was the first time I became painfully aware of the cost to others, not just to myself. I reflected back on the job that I left because I did not know how to ask for help after I was promoted beyond my capabilities. I thought of all the friends and sweethearts that I left behind because I was not willing to tell the truth about what I felt or wanted. I also thought of other times I did express myself, but I spoke with venom because I waited so long to say anything that I was ready to explode. I thought of all that, and I made a commitment to myself that I would change.

PowerPhrases are one result of that commitment. I collect words and phrases that have impact. They help me to speak when speaking is appropriate and they help me to speak so people can hear. I remember times in the past when a situation screamed for comment and the words did not come. PowerPhrases keep me from being tongue-tied anymore.

Now I am a professional speaker, and I gather and give out PowerPhrases at my presentations. My audiences love them, and so will you.

I never imagined I would write a book like this one. I was always a "grow from the inside out" kind of person. PowerPhrases grow you from the outside in. Of course, what really matters is simply that we keep growing at all.

Knowing exactly what to say does not solve all communication and assertiveness problems—but it does provide tremendous help.

INTRODUCTION

A Toolbox of Perfect Expressions

Have you ever needed to express yourself but did not because you could not find the right words? Have you ever walked away from a situation and thought of the perfect thing to say AFTER it was too late? Have you ever given long explanations and wondered—is there a faster, more effective way to communicate?

PowerPhrases! is the answer to these problems and questions. *PowerPhrases!* provides a toolbox of the perfect expressions to get your point across clearly and confidently. This book provides powerful words when you need them the most. You will learn the exact words to use to:

- Assure common understanding.
- Clear up conflict.
- Establish a connection.
- Get what you want.
- Refuse what you don't want.

Knowing what to say results in:

- Increased confidence.
- Enhanced self-esteem.
- Refinement and professionalism.
- The ability to slide out of sticky situations with grace and ease.

While many books tell you what approach to take in addressing challenging situations, *PowerPhrases!* tells you exactly what to say.

Power Pointer

Few people understand what true power is. True power is not power over anyone or anything. True power is the ability to influence and the ability to get things done. True power in communication is found when the communication gets the results you seek.

Take a look at the roots of the word communication. It comes from the word communion. Communication is effective when it builds a bridge between speaker and listener.

If you are looking for a book to give you power over others, PowerPhrases! is not it. If you are looking for a book to help you build bridges and dissolve barriers, this is the book for you.

How to Use PowerPhrases!

1. Read through *PowerPhrases!* cover to cover at least once to get an overview of what a PowerPhrase is. Then read it again to select the PowerPhrases you like and that are most useful to you. I have highlighted and bulleted the PowerPhrases so you can find them with ease. Memorize them. Put them on your fridge, next to your bed and on your bathroom mirror. Practice them until they become automatic. Better yet, practice using them with a role-play partner. Have someone play a person you need to address while you practice your PowerPhrases. You'll find that the words will come more easily if you have practiced them in a safe environment.
2. Use *PowerPhrases!* as a reference when you prepare to face a challenging situation. Look up the situation and learn the key phrases that make sense to you.
3. Whenever you have a situation that does not go as well as you want, return to the book and pick what you wish you had said. The PowerPhrase will be ready to use the next time.

Power Tip– Here's a Pointer for Sounding Calm.

Pretend you are asking your listener to pass the butter. Asking for the butter is not highly emotional, right? Your vocal tone is calm. That's the tone to use when you communicate your PowerPhrases.

Be Prepared to Experience Life at a New Level

Whether your habit is to over-express or under-express, be prepared for exciting changes when you communicate with PowerPhrases. Get ready to experience richness in your relationships. That is a natural result of good communication.

The PowerPhrases in this book are here to help you express more of who you are in the world. These are the things you would have said all along, if you had only known how to.

PowerPhrases to the Rescue

I coached Sandy through a tough relationship and divorce. Sandy was intimidated by her domineering spouse. She would be alternately combative and apologetic with him.

One day she called to tell me about how she had communicated her anger with her estranged husband because he had cashed a check that was hers, and kept the money. Sandy was feeling guilty about "hurting" him and about how she expressed her anger. I was sympathetic when we began the conversation, but after she told me what she had said, I informed her that her guilt was misplaced. Her anger was appropriate and she communicated it responsibly. What I thought was really going on was that she was communicating with a new power that was unfamiliar to her. She was frightened by her own power. Her desire to apologize was, in fact, a retreat into a more familiar submissive stance. If you are not used to being your own advocate, PowerPhrases can seem cruel and harsh. If you are accustomed to overreacting, PowerPhrases can seem mushy and soft. Either way requires adjusting to a powerful new way of communicating.

CHAPTER 1

PowerPhrases™ Defined: What Is a PowerPhrase Anyway?

Let's get some help from the dictionary.

- Power is the ability to get results.
- A phrase is a short, colorful expression.

Therefore a PowerPhrase is:

- A short, colorful expression that gets results.

The results come when you say what you mean, mean what you say, and are not being mean when you say it.

This leads to the following definition:

PowerPhrase: A short colorful expression that gets results by saying what you mean, meaning what you say, and not being mean when you say it.

PowerPhrase: A short colorful expression that gets results by saying what you mean, meaning what you say, and not being mean when you say it.

A PowerPhrase is a SHORT Expression

- **Less is more!**

Say it and stop talking! Forget the detailed explanations that sound like apologies and suggest that you do not have a right to your position. For example, if someone asks you to run for club president and you do not want to, don't say:

— *You know, it is really great that you asked me to serve, and I want to tell you how much I appreciate it! This is the first time anyone has made me an offer like this. Really, ordinarily I would love to, but under the circumstances…*

Instead, use a **PowerPhrase for Saying No**, such as:

- **I'm flattered you asked. My decision is to not serve at this time.**
- **Thanks for asking. I choose not to serve.**
- **I would be happy to if I had the time. I make a policy of not over-scheduling myself, and this would overload my schedule.**

Martin Luther King, Jr. understood the importance of being brief when he said,

- **"I have a dream!"**

A longer phrase such as:

— *I have some really good ideas that inspire me and I think you'll want to listen.*

does not carry the impact and is not a PowerPhrase.

PowerPhrases grab your attention and create pictures in your mind.

PowerPhrases Are COLORFUL Expressions.

Have you ever been deeply moved by the hook to a song?

- **"Love will turn you around."**

Have you ever been inspired by an advertising or political slogan?

- **"Just do it!"**

and

- **"Count every vote!"**

Has a catch phrase ever helped you to understand a concept?

- **"Put first things first." (Stephen Covey)**

These expressions are colorful. They grab your attention and create pictures in your mind. What adds to their color is that they carry the essence of the message and exclude words that weaken the impact. Be as brief as possible in your expression.

PowerPhrases Get RESULTS

Consciously choose what results you want to achieve. If your conscious mind does not set a goal for the conversation, your unconscious mind will. I am amazed at how often people speak in a way that alienates the very person who can help them. Consider these questions in every conversation you have.

1. How can I get what I want?
2. How do I preserve the relationship while getting what I want?

Weigh both values and choose words that address both.

PowerPhrases Say What You Mean

It sounds simple enough. But do you really say what you mean? Or do you avoid clarity to avoid a reaction? Perhaps you say:

— *That's okay. Don't worry about it.*

When a **PowerPhrase for Addressing Conflict** would be more effective. Consider these:

- **This is a problem. We need to find a solution.**
- **This is unacceptable and needs to be addressed.**
- **I need your help to resolve this.**

If your conscious mind does not set a goal for the conversation, your unconscious mind will.

With PowerPhrases You Mean What You Say!

Do you mean what you say? Or do you say:

- **I will…(start the meetings on time whether you are here or not.)**

And then when that person is late you wait to begin.

Everyone knows when your deadlines aren't real. Everyone knows when your resistance can be overcome. Everyone knows when you do not intend to follow through! PowerPhrases are as powerful as your commitment to them. In the words of Emerson:

- **"What you do speaks so loudly I cannot hear a thing you say."**

Do not say something unless you intend to back yourself up with action.

You must back up your words with actions.

This can be hard! Have you ever told a coworker what time you could meet and they pressured you to meet with them immediately? What did you do? Yield to their pressure or stand firm with what you said? You must back your words up with actions. If the guilt monster starts whispering recriminations in your ear, remind yourself that your needs are important too.

Power Pointer— Mean What You Say

Claudia would consistently tell her boss how important it was for her to leave work on time, and she told him what she needed from him in order for that to happen. Her boss would ignore her requests and she would stay late to make sure everything was completed.

Then Claudia had a change in childcare that made it impossible for her to stay more than fifteen minutes past her regular work times. Her boss was upset the first time she left before the work was complete, but he quickly learned that now Claudia meant what she said about leaving on time. Miraculously, now that there was a cost to him for not getting things to her, he began to get her what she needed so that she was able to complete her work by end of the business day.

PowerPhrases are as powerful as your commitment to them.

PowerPhrases Avoid Being Mean

Are you being mean in how you say it? PowerPhrases (1) avoid sarcasm, (2) overkill, (3) assumption of guilt and (4) an attempt to overpower the other person with wit.

1. PowerPhrases Avoid Sarcasm.

— *Look who decided to show up…*

is NOT a PowerPhrase.

- **When you come late it throws off my schedule for the rest of the day. How can I help you to get here on time?**

is a PowerPhrase.

Sarcasm is indirect. PowerPhrases are direct. Sarcasm mocks the listener. PowerPhrases honor the listener. One definition of sarcasm is "the tearing of flesh."

2. PowerPhrases Avoid Overkill.

A PowerPhrase is as strong as it needs to be and no stronger. A PowerPhrase does not shoot a cannon when a BB would work. For example:

- **Absolutely not!**

can be a PowerPhrase, but only when a gentler version such as:

- **Not this time. Thanks for asking.**

does not work.

3. PowerPhrases Avoid Assumption of Guilt.

PowerPhrases assume positive intentions unless it is proven otherwise. Avoid the accusative voice of "you language." Say:

PowerPhrases avoid the assumption of guilt.

- **I am getting angry.**

Rather than:

— *You make me so mad!*

Say:

- **I was promised a commission structure six months ago and I still do not have one. If this is not resolved I will…**

rather than:

— *You lied!*

4. PowerPhrases Avoid Attempts to Outsmart the Other Person With Wit.

If the boss asks "What kind of idiot are you?" you might be tempted to say:

— *The same kind of idiot as the person who hired me.*

— *You tell me. You are the obvious expert.*

Are they clever responses? Yes. Are they PowerPhrases? No. People who use PowerPhrases speak to obtain powerful results. Instead, use the PowerPhrase:

- **When you ask, "What kind of idiot are you?" I find it insulting. I prefer you offer solutions when I make mistakes.**

Power Tip— Speak up EARLY!

When you express yourself as soon as things become a problem, you minimize the likelihood that you will overreact.

Kris and Carol were on a team in a job that required them to set up displays. Kris thought Carol always undid any display she arranged and she resented it. Carol didn't know there was a problem until the end of a week of working together when she overheard an indirect remark Kris made to someone else. She was surprised to discover what a villain she had become!

Because Kris hadn't spoken up, what began as a few rearranged books became an issue of power and control. We have all done this. Speak up early!

When you speak up as soon as things become a problem, you minimize the likelihood that you will overreact.

Now that you understand the characteristics of PowerPhrases, practice the exercises below. Then read Chapter 2 to see how PowerPhrases can overcome killer phrases.

Exercise — The PowerPhrase Questions

PowerPhrase wisdom says, before you speak, ask yourself;

1. Is it short?
2. Is it colorful?
3. Is it likely to get positive results?
4. Does it truly say what I mean?
5. Do I intend to back my words with action?
6. Am I being kind in my choice of words?

List your favorite phrases below.

____

____

____

Next, apply the above questions to your phrases.

If all of your answers are yes, your phrases are PowerPhrases! If you get any "nos", find a better expression in the chapters of this book.

For example, a common phrase among teenagers is "Whatever."

1. Is it short? Yes!
2. Is it colorful? I believe so.
3. Is it likely to get positive results? No. It is likely to create resentment and resistance.
4. Does it truly say what you mean? It conveys very little information.
5. Do you intend to back the message up with action? The message does not imply a clear position to back up.
6. Are you being kind in your choice of words? No. Usually this expression is intended sarcastically.

Eliminate the powerless phrases and fill your vocabulary with PowerPhrases. Read on to chapter 3 for more tools in recognizing PowerPhrases when you hear them.

CHAPTER 2

Killer Phrases and the PowerPhrases™ to Overcome Them

It is essential that you learn to recognize a PowerPhrase when you hear it, and know the difference between PowerPhrases and "killer phrases." There are nine types of killer phrases. They include (1) filler killer phrases, (2) indecisive killer phrases, (3) deflective killer phrases, (4) negative killer phrases, (5) absolute killer phrases, (6) victim killer phrases, (7) vague hinting killer phrases, (8) emotional killer phrases and, (9) passive killer phrases.

Throughout this book you will see examples of all of these phrases applied in different settings with the PowerPhrases to overcome them. This chapter gives you the overview you need to spot powerless and powerful communication anywhere in life.

There are nine types of killer phrases.

1. Avoid Killer Fillers.

Qualifiers, hedges and softener phrases can weaken the intended message. Avoid the following phrases:

— *Well...*

— *Sort of...*

— *I just...*

— *I would tend to...*

— *I guess...*

— *I kind of…*

— *You know…*

— *I'm wondering if…*

— *I'm not sure about this but…*

— *I could be wrong but…*

— *This is just my opinion, but…*

— *Sorry to bother you but…*

Tag phrases also weaken your messages. Tag phrases are expressions that you tack on to the end of what you say that turn your statement into a question. For example, if you say:

- **This is the best proposal…**

and you follow with:

Tag phrases weaken your messages.

— *You know?*

— *Isn't it?*

— *Right?*

— *Do you see?*

you imply that you are not sure and need the other person's verification. Other weakening tags are:

— *Aren't you?*

— *Doesn't it?*

— *Won't you?*

If the statement really is a question, follow the statement with a clear and direct question.

Also, eliminate all words that do not add useful information. Kind of like… you know?

Power Pointer — Join Toastmasters International

To eliminate filler words, I recommend that you attend Toastmasters International meetings. When you speak, someone will count the number of filler words that you use. Most people are quite surprised to learn how many ums and uhs they are saying. Becoming conscious is the first step in making a change. Initially people get very self-conscious about having their filler words counted, but gradually the habit is broken.

2. Replace Indecisive Killer Phrases With Decisive PowerPhrases.

Speak with certainty and decisiveness. If you cannot be certain on one position, express what you can be certain about.

Speak with certainty and decisiveness.

Avoid	Replace with
I should…	I will…
I'll try…	I will…
I might be able to…	What I can commit to is…
I sort of think…	I know…
It's just my opinion…	I believe…
I would tend to think…	I think…
You might want to consider…	I recommend…

Do not doubt yourself! Speak what you know with confidence. If your words express doubt, your listener will doubt you no matter how true your words are.

Learn the power of "I will" rather than "I'll try."

PowerPhrases to the Rescue

I have an email friendship with a dear old friend who is quite successful in his career. We agreed that we wanted to have a phone conversation and he would tell me "I'll try to call you next week." When the phone call didn't come I would fill him in on my upcoming schedule. Once again he would promise to "try" to call but the call never came. This happened several times.

I was reluctant to confront him about it, because I saw him as important and busy and I was afraid I might anger him. When I noticed I felt undervalued I realized I needed to speak. I said:

- **I would rather forget about our having a phone conversation, than for you to say that you will try, and then have it not happen. I feel let down and undervalued, as if our friendship is not important to you. Let's not talk about speaking on the phone until you are able to tell me what you will do rather than what you will try to do.**

He responded with an apology and a firm commitment to a day and time, which he upheld. We had a wonderful conversation. I was reminded of the power of asking for what I want—and the power of "I will" rather than "I'll try."

3. Replace Killer Phrases That Deflect Due Credit and Replace Them With PowerPhrases That Accept Due Credit.

When was the last time you deflected a compliment? Yesterday? I am not suggesting you brag. Bragging does not impress anyone–but neither does false modesty.

Avoid	Replace with
I got lucky.	I worked hard.
It was nothing…	Thanks for noticing.
This old thing?	Thank you.
Anyone could have…	I'm pleased with the outcome too.

When you deflect a compliment, you are refusing a gift. Accept their gifts and do not play small.

Bragging does not impress anyone—but neither does false modesty.

Power Pointer–Accept Due Credit.

Did you know that women are far more likely to deflect compliments and credit for their accomplishments than men are?

I saw this point illustrated when I was receiving cranial sacral treatment from a husband/wife team. (Cranial sacral is a type of bodywork.) When I came for the second treatment, the husband asked what results I had experienced from the first one. I said it seemed like it was a good thing to do. He asked if my shoulder pain was better, and I replied that it was, but I had thought that was due to not having been on the computer. He and his wife spoke simultaneously. He said, " I think we deserve credit for that." At the exact same moment his wife said "Oh, that's probably it."

Accept credit when due!

4. Replace Negative Killer Phrases With Positive PowerPhrases

Be careful of negative killer phrases. You know the ones. Do not get so focused on what you do not want that that's all you can think about. That leaves no room for what you want!

Your mind makes sense of positives more easily than negatives. Put your focus on what you want, not on what you do not want. Talk about how you will solve a problem or what you learned from a mistake more than you talk about the problem. Draw attention to your strengths, taking the focus off your weaknesses.

Your mind makes sense of positives more easily than negatives.

Avoid	Replace with
Everything went wrong…	I learned from some setbacks.
I'll have to…	I'll be glad to…
I can't…	What I can do is…
I am spending time…	I am investing time…
I'm no good at…	I'm getting better at…
You'll have to excuse…	Here it is…
If only I had…	Starting now I will…
This is bad…	What good can we get out of this?
I can't get to this until…	I can get to this by…
Don't forget to…(log off of your computer.)	Be certain to…(log off of your computer.)

Any time you find yourself ready to express a negative, ask yourself what the upside is and speak from that perspective.

Power Thinking–Think in the Positive

One day as I was walking up to address a group in Amarillo, Texas, I was thinking,

— "Don't call it armadillo. Don't call it armadillo."

When I opened my mouth what came out was,

— "I am delighted to be here in armadillo."

My subconscious did not register the "don't", and armadillo was imprinted on my brain. Next time I will remind myself of what I DO want to say.

- **It's Amarillo.**

5. Replace Absolute Killer Phrases and Labels With Accurate PowerPhrases

You lose credibility when you speak in sweeping generalizations and absolutes.

You lose credibility when you speak in sweeping generalizations and absolutes. Stick to the facts! "Always" and "never" are generalizations that are rarely factual.

Avoid	Replace with
You always…	On several occasions you have…
I never…	Up until now I have not…
Everything…	Many things…
You're lazy.	Your performance is not up to standard.
You are incompetent.	There are several mistakes here that need to be fixed.

Support your assertions with specific examples.

6. Replace Victim Killer Phrases With PowerPhrases That Place Responsibility and Emphasis Where it is Due

You do not score any points or gain any credit for indicating that you are someone else's victim.

— *Poor me!*

is not a PowerPhrase. Any statement that inappropriately places responsibility on others is not a PowerPhrase either. Don't say:

— *You make me so mad.*

— *You make me feel wonderful!*

When you say that, you are saying that you have no control over your own emotions. That is not the message that you want to send. Do not imply that you do not have the ability to choose alternative thoughts and behaviors.

If you make your feelings the subject when the real subject is something else, you sound immature and childish.

It is often recommended that you replace an accusative sounding "you" statement with "I" statements, such as:

- **I feel angry when you…**
- **I feel wonderful when you…**

Notice that these statements avoid placing responsibility for the emotion on the other person. While that is good, there can be a problem in that they make your feelings the subject of the communication. If you make your feelings the subject when the real subject is something else, you sound immature and childish. If the subject of your communication is your anger or wonderful feelings, the above statements are appropriate and accurate PowerPhrases. If the subject is something else, the above statements are not PowerPhrases.

If the point you want to make is that Joe's tardiness causes you all kinds of problems, do not make Joe or yourself the subject of the communication. Rather than saying:

— *You make me mad when you come late.*

or:

— *I get angry when you are late.*

Use a **PowerPhrase to Place Responsibility and Emphasis Where it is Due**, such as:

- **Starting late causes serious problems and needs to be addressed.**

Do not say:

— *Traffic made me late. (Accusatory. The traffic may not care, but you do not sound powerful.)*

Instead use a **PowerPhrase to Place Responsibility and Emphasis Where it is Due**, such as:

- **There was more traffic than I allowed for.**

Do not say:

— *You are not being clear. (Accusatory)*

— *I am not following you. (Makes you the subject.)*

Instead use a **PowerPhrase to Place Responsibility and Emphasis Where it is Due**, such as:

- **Please clarify this point.**
- **That last point is not clear to me.**

Simply ask yourself what you are really talking about, and make that the subject.

7. Replace Hints and Vague Killer Phrases With Specific PowerPhrases.

Have you ever hinted to someone and then been upset because they did not take your hint? Be straightforward and specific about what you want. You have only yourself to blame if people do not respond to your vague requests.

Be straightforward and specific about what you want.

Avoid	Replace with
I sure wish someone would…	Will you…
I'd like to have something like…	I want ___ by___ because___.
You need to do a better job.	Your performance needs to be improved. Here are the criteria for acceptable performance. Number one…

Do you hint at things in order to avoid risking rejection? If you never clearly ask, you will never be turned down! Powerful people are willing to risk rejection for the sake of clarity and effectiveness.

8. Avoid Emotional Killer Phrases in Business Situations Where Factual Action–Based PowerPhrases Hold More Power.

Stick to information and action phrases.

Your emotions are important. However, there is a good chance that the person you are communicating with is far less concerned with your emotions than you are, and far more interested in facts and outcomes. You are usually better off when you stick to information and action phrases.

Know what you feel. Find people to communicate your frustrations and hurts to. Then choose PowerPhrases that are factual and action based.

Avoid	Replace with
I feel great about this proposal.	This proposal will improve our bottom line by ___.
I don't like this idea.	There are three serious problems with this idea. First…
I am angry about this delay.	How do you plan to get back on schedule after this delay?

9. Avoid Passive Killer Phrases and Replace With Active PowerPhrases.

What is wrong with the following sentence?

"The acquisition contract was signed by the CFO."

This statement is in the passive voice. You can tell a passive sentence by the inclusion of "was," which is a form of the verb "to be." This sentence starts with the contract, even though the CFO is the one acting and should be the subject. To be in the active voice, the sentence needs to begin with the one acting.

Avoid	Replace with
The acquisition contract was signed by the CFO.	**The CFO signed the acquisition contract.**
The bone was buried by the dog.	**The dog buried the bone.**

You will develop perceptiveness for PowerPhrases that will work like radar.

Overcome Killer Phrases With PowerPhrases

Keep your eyes open to see how the principles of this chapter are applied everywhere. When you understand the principles of PowerPhrases and are familiar with the specific applications in other chapters, you will develop perceptiveness that will work like radar. You will immediately recognize the difference between killer phrases and PowerPhrases.

Exercise

Replace the following killer phrases with PowerPhrases.

I sort of like this idea.

____

This is just my opinion, but...

____

This is great, don't you think?

____

I might be able to...

____

It was no big deal.

____

Don't come late.

____

This will never work.

____

You hurt my feelings.

____

I wish I didn't have to go to the meeting alone.

____

I'm excited about this account.

____

The suspect was apprehended.

____

Chapter 3

PowerPhrases™ for Saying "No"
"No" Is a Complete Sentence – But Is It a PowerPhrase?

"No" is so short, so simple, and so powerful. "No" also can be so frightening. When was the last time you agreed to something because you were afraid to say no?

According to informal polls I conduct, two-thirds of the population has trouble with that little two-letter word! PowerPhrases make saying "no" easier.

Nancy Reagan knew the importance of having the right words to say when she began an anti-drug campaign based on the slogan "Just say:

- **No!"**

to drugs. Other phrases such as:

- **"NO is a complete sentence!"**

and

- **"What part of NO don't you understand?"**

evolved from this campaign.

Two-thirds of the population has trouble saying no.

While powerful, these phrases are flat refusals. Flat refusals carry risk and are not always appropriate.

A flat refusal can brand you as rude and uncooperative. A flat refusal may be interpreted as discrediting the request or offer. While a flat refusal does say what it means and mean what it says, it can come across as being hostile.

PowerPhrases use the amount of power required and no more. Start gently and work your way up if necessary.

There are three steps for saying no.

The Three-Step Process for Saying "No"

When You Refuse a Request, ACT!

1. **Acknowledge** their request.

Say something to recognize their request. Make a short comment to let them know that you heard them and you are considering what they said.

2. Clarify your **Circumstance.**

Tell them a little bit about your own situation. You do not need to be specific. You will want to be very brief. Mention what it is that keeps you from being able to honor their request.

A flat refusal can brand you as rude and uncooperative.

3. **Transform** your refusal into a positive. Suggest alternatives or make a comment that reaffirms the relationship.

For example, consider:

- **It sounds like a great idea. Unfortunately I have other priorities. Perhaps next time I can.**

This includes all three elements.

Step 1: Acknowledge — PowerPhrases to Acknowledge the Request

- **I understand this is important.**
- **Ordinarily I would love to help.**
- **I appreciate you thinking of me.**
- **Thanks for asking.**
- **I wish I could help out here.**
- **I am aware…**
- **What a great idea!**

- I am flattered you asked.
- I understand your situation. I have been there myself.

Step 2: Circumstances — PowerPhrases to Explain Circumstances

- My situation is…
- My policy is…
- I have plans.
- I'm not up to it.
- I'm not the best person for this job.
- I'm not available.
- I have commitments.
- It doesn't work for me.
- My circumstances make it impossible.
- After realizing the scope…
- I choose not to.
- I will pass on this opportunity.
- I am responsible for…

When you refuse a request, ACT!

Step 3: Transform — PowerPhrases to Transform the Refusal by Reaffirming the Relationship or Offering Alternatives

- Perhaps next time.
- Thanks again for asking.
- I hope you can find the help you need.
- I wish I could.
- While I can't do what you are asking, what I can do is…
- Here's an alternative…
- Have you considered…?
- Have you tried asking Judy? (While this might work

for you, it also might not make you very popular with Judy.)

- **I can help you by…**

ACT Now! Put the Three-Step Process for Saying "No" Together to Get Complete PowerPhrases.

Combine one phrase from each of the three categories to make a complete and effective **PowerPhrase for Saying "No"** without caving in and without losing friends.

Say "No" without caving in and without losing friends.

Acknowledge	Circumstances	Transform
I understand this is important.	My situation is ...	Perhaps next time.
Ordinarily I would love to help.	My policy is ...	Thanks for asking.
I appreciate you thinking of me.	I have other plans...	I'm sure you'll find the right person you need.
I would if I could.	I have other involvements.	Have you considered..?
I wish I could help out here.	I'm not well-suited to do what you want.	Here's an option...
I see you need help.	After looking at my calendar I see I can't give you the help you need.	Have you considered asking ___?
I'm honored that you thought of me.	After realizing the scope of the request, I chose to pass.	I wish you success.

Liberated by a Two Letter Word and Some Good Healthy Power Thinking

I was on a team with "Mike," whom I found to be controlling. It seemed to me that I was constantly giving in, but I did not worry about it because the issues were small and I was able to go along. That changed when Mike expected me to split a bill that was his responsibility. Although it was only an issue of about five dollars, I knew that if I paid it, I would not feel good about myself.

I used the ACT formula and stood my ground. He was quite used to getting his way, and became visibly upset when I did not cave in to his pressure. After I "ACTed" him four times, he paid the bill and we walked down the hallway in silence. He was bristly and cold, and I was thinking:

— *Oh Meryl, what have you done? Now he will be impossible to work with. Am I being picky? It's not that much money.*

Then I heard myself and I said to myself:

- **Meryl, you have a habit of being unhappy when other people are upset with you. Get over it!**

In that moment I was free. He was unhappy with me-and I was quite pleased with myself. I see bondage as being constrained by other people's opinions of us. Freedom is being our own judge and jury.

Later that day Mike did something else that I thought was outrageous, and I "ACTed" once more. Now it was becoming easier.

Not everyone will appreciate your use of PowerPhrases. You will appreciate yourself.

Freedom is being our own judge and jury.

Avoid being too specific and wordy. Don't say:

— *Gosh, I am so sorry, I really hate to tell you this because it sounds like you could use some help and I would love to help you if I could. If only the circumstances were different, but I have to take my daughter to little league and last time I missed a game I felt just awful because (etc.)...*

The more details you give, the weaker you sound and the more inclined they will be to argue.

Sometimes they will argue even when you are clear and direct. In these cases, use only two of the three parts to add strength to your "no."

Saying "No" in Two Parts

The more details you give, the weaker you sound and the more inclined they will be to argue.

When you say no in two parts, it can sound stronger. Some people's sensitivity causes them to hear the slightest hint of "no" as a personal rejection and they need a softer version. Use all three steps for them. Others do not take it as personally, and a two-part no works well.

There are some people that will argue with and attempt to manipulate anything we say. A two-part no works better with these.

The Two-Step Process for Saying "No"

Acknowledge	Circumstances	Transform
I'd love to.	However, I am busy.	
Thanks for asking.	Not this time.	
	My boss has already scheduled my time.	If you want, you can ask her.
Sounds interesting.	I have other commitments.	
	I have a 3:00 deadline.	I wish I could.

Power Thinking to the Rescue

What are you telling yourself that keeps you from saying "no"? Don't think:

- *If I say no, they may not like me.*
- *I better be nice.*
- *I shouldn't say what I think.*

Instead, use Power Thinking. Think:

- **What are my true priorities?**
- **What response best serves my true priorities?**
- **How can I communicate that as graciously and effectively as possible?**

People who are comfortable saying no are usually people who have a clear idea of what their priorities are. Use Power Thinking to remind you of yours.

People who are comfortable saying no are usually people who have a clear idea of what their priorities are.

When a Simple "NO" Is a PowerPhrase

As you recall, a PowerPhrase is as strong as it needs to be, and no stronger. A PowerPhrase does not shoot a cannon when a BB would work. In addition, a PowerPhrase assumes good intentions unless it is proven otherwise.

The fact is, sometimes people simply do not get the message on the first communication. Stronger PowerPhrases can be called for when:

1. The listener is unusually direct,
2. The listener is manipulative or a "taker", or
3. The listener hears acknowledgement as uncertainty or as an opening.

For example, Jan is naturally very direct. She expects and appreciates directness from others. Jan appreciates a flat no. She does not want to take the time to hear all the reasons. "No" is a PowerPhrase for her.

Roberta is a nurse who works in a hospital. She will take advantage of others when they allow it. None of the staff enjoy working weekends, but it is a supportive environment where people pitch in for each other. When Roberta asked Jan to take her weekend shift, Jan assumed Roberta had a great need, and agreed. She felt used when she later discovered that Roberta did not have anything special happening, she simply did not want to work weekends. The next time Roberta asked her to cover her shift, Jan said:

Acknowledge	Circumstances	Transform
"I am aware you don't enjoy working weekends.	My family likes me home weekends as well. My policy is to cover for people only when they have emergencies."	

A PowerPhrase is as strong as it needs to be, and no stronger.

That statement is a PowerPhrase; strong, clear and direct.

Roberta started having a lot of "emergencies." Jan used another approach. She tried to turn the "no" into a negotiation by saying:

Acknowledge	Circumstances	Transform
"I understand you don't want to work weekends.	I will happy to cover for you again after you have covered a weekend for me"	

Although Jan was being strong, clear and direct, Roberta saw it as an opportunity to argue. "Well, I did cover for you a couple of weekdays in trade for your weekend. I wanted to cover for you the other weekend, but you didn't want to take that weekend off." Jan realized that with Roberta, her PowerPhrase was to just say:

- **No.**

or

- **No, I do not want to.**

and to refuse to discuss it any further. Roberta tested Jan's no: Jan had to repeat it several times. Eventually Roberta gave up and found someone else to take advantage of. If you have ever tried to assert yourself with someone who argues with any explanation you give, you probably already know that with these people it is best to avoid explanations that give them something to argue about.

Turning a NO Into a Negotiation

Sometimes, rather than completely refusing a request or offer, suggest alternatives. For example, when one assistant was asked to make copies, she said she would love to but she had a huge stack of orders to file. Then she used the PowerPhrase:

Sometimes, rather than completely refusing a request or offer, suggest alternatives.

- **I'll do it if you'll...(help file orders).**

Another assistant's boss gave her an assignment that would require her full attention. She said:

Acknowledge	Circumstances	Transform
"I know this project is top priority.	In order to meet the deadline I need to have uninterrupted time.	I can do this if you'll answer the phones."

Her supervisor answered the phones for her for two weeks, because it was necessary to get the job done.

Many business people know how to say "no" to their bosses without ever using the word. When a supervisor makes a request that conflicts with a previous request, they will reply:

Acknowledge	Circumstances	Transform
"I know this is important.	I am working on the XYZ account.	Which is the priority?
		What can I put aside to make time to complete this?"

PowerPhrases That Buy You Time

If you are a chronic yes-sayer, you can overcome the yes habit by using a PowerPhrase to delay long enough to plan your response.

A chronic yes–sayer can overcome the habit by using PowerPhrases to buy time.

Delay phrases lack the power of a clear refusal, but are superior to a yes when you do not mean it. Learn the **PowerPhrases for Buying Time.**

- **Let me get back to you.**
- **I need to check on a few things before answering you.**
- **I need to give this consideration before responding.**
- **Let me think about it and let you know.**
- **I'll see what I can do and tell you tomorrow.**

When you use these, be sure to mean what you say. Check on, consider or think about it, and get back to them. Do not let it remain unresolved.

When They Ask, "Will You Do Me a Favor?"

What do you say when someone asks you to agree before telling you what the request is? Don't say:

— *Sure.*

Instead, use a **PowerPhrase for Getting Clarification Before Agreeing,** such as:

- **What do you need?**

- **I just might! What is it?**
- **Tell me what and I'll see.**
- **I need to know what the favor is before I can answer you.**

PowerPhrases to the Rescue—Before You Agree...

When I train assistants I share a story about a woman who was an assistant for a VP in her company. At a convention, the CEO of the company came to her and said, "Wouldn't it be nice if we had hats with the company logo embroidered on them for all 650 employees this evening? Please take care of that."

The CEO had never made a request of this woman before, so he was not aware of her history of excellence.

Her response was to say, "I have no idea of how I could possibly do that." That response had negative repercussions for her.

At seminars I have my groups explore options. Some ask for clarification of budget, quality specifications and if the evening meeting is an absolute deadline. Others ACT by acknowledging the great idea, explaining why they believe it might not be possible and suggesting alternatives. Still others buy time, and say:

- **Let me check on a few things and get back to you.**

Learning to say no does not mean that we ignore the sensitivities of the other person. It does mean that we also respect our own requirements.

Learning to say no does not mean that we ignore the sensitivities of the other person.

EXERCISES

I. You have been asked to do something that falls outside of your direct line of work and expertise. How do you refuse the assignment?

Step 1:

Acknowledge the request.

____

Step 2:

Explain **Circumstances**

____

Step 3:

Transform the refusal into a positive by reaffirming the relationship or suggesting an alternative.

____

II. Someone is taking a collection for a birthday gift for an employee you don't know. You are on a tight budget. How do you refuse?

Step 1:

Acknowledge the request.

____

Step 2:

Explain **Circumstances**

____

Step 3:

Transform the refusal into a positive by reaffirming the relationship or suggesting an alternative.

____

The Power of NO

The Beatles wrote a song that contains the following lines: "I ain't no fool and I don't take what I don't want." Every time you say "yes" to something you don't want, you are saying "no" to what you do. As with any habit, overcoming the "yes" habit will be uncomfortable. Say no anyway! Take a deep breath and use the "butter" voice that was described in the introduction. Whatever you do, do not take your words back because you are outside of your comfort zone.

I often meet people who used to say yes, and have since discovered the power of no. They found it a challenge at first, but incredibly rewarding. They always smile when they tell me about saying no, because the small and powerful word helps them take control and sets them free. These PowerPhrases will help YOU take control and they will set you free.

Chapter 4

PowerPhrases™ That Transform Conflicts Into Understanding

What words come to mind when you think of conflict? Write four below.

____________________ ____________________

____________________ ____________________

My audiences often pick words like anger, frustration, shouting, and tension. What do these words have in common? They are all negative! Can you think of some positive words that apply to conflict? Write four below.

____________________ ____________________

____________________ ____________________

Train yourself to think Power Thoughts and to speak PowerPhrases in conflict.

Was that a bit harder? It usually is. It is challenging to think of words like breakthrough, understanding, and resolution. You will have to train yourself to think Power Thoughts and to speak PowerPhrases in conflict. Negative words and statements that intensify the conflict come more easily.

It will help if you view conflict as a natural and healthy aspect of life and relationships. This attitude helps you become more willing to air your differences at earlier stages, and that makes resolution much easier.

Think: "There is a solution here."

Power Thinking to the Rescue

Pay attention to your thoughts when conflict begins. Don't think:

— I better avoid this disagreement.

— I can't handle conflict.

— Who do they think they are?

Instead, choose Power Thoughts, such as:

- **There is a solution here.**
- **Conflict is a normal part of life and we will get to the other side.**
- **I can stay calm and express myself gracefully.**
- **What do I want? What do they want? How can we resolve this?**

About a year ago, I was contracted by the Department of Defense to do three days of conflict management training. The entire division was called in for the training because a few men had had incidences of violence. None of them wanted to be there. They tried to get the unions to stop the training. This was the most hostile group I have ever faced.

I had to be very assertive with myself about my thinking. I was tempted to think:

— This is going to be awful!

— I want out of here!

— I can't handle this.

Every time I had a thought like that, I chose to replace the thought with Power Thoughts such as:

- **I am very good at what I do.**
- **This is an opportunity.**

- **They are going to be very glad that this training was mandatory.**

By the end they were very glad to have been there. I had Power Thinking to thank.

Conflict is a very hot topic! Do you want to know how to get that other person to shape up? Do you want to know exactly what to say to put others in their place? This chapter will not tell you either. What it will do is tell you exactly what to say to keep from being the source of the problem, and give you concrete steps and phrases to use to resolve the problems that do occur.

When conflicts arise, you must know how to make your CASE! That means:

Clarify their position,

Assert your own,

Seek solutions and

Evaluate options and create agreements.

When conflicts arise, make your CASE.

Make your CASE Step 1: Clarifying Their Position

Do you ever jump to conclusions in conflict situations? Do you imagine that they are doing awful things on purpose? Do you think they are out to get you? If so, you are normal! We all become overly self-focused, and we reach conclusions before clear evidence is obtained. Develop a habit of standing in the other person's shoes. Clarify their perspective before asserting your own.

Dr. Stephen Covey says to:

- **"Seek first to understand and then to be understood."**

Adopt this motto–with one addition.

- **Seek first to understand, and make it clear to them that you do. Then seek to be understood.**

It is not enough that you understand the other person. They need to feel understood. Remember that:

- **No one cares how much you know until they know how much you care.**[1]

It is not enough that you understand the other person. They need to feel understood.

Power Listening to the Rescue

The meeting was getting nowhere. Sheila was on the defensive. Whatever people said was considered to be a personal affront.

Finally I said:

- **I suggest that we listen to Sheila and tell her our understanding of what she is saying until we are certain and she is certain that we are hearing her.**

The suggestion worked like magic. Sheila relaxed and spoke from a position of being open and vulnerable. Surprisingly, once she had the floor, she only needed to speak a short while. Then she was open to hearing what we had to say.

You will get excellent results when you demonstrate interest and concern as the first step in managing conflict. Explore your assumptions by asking questions. Ask your questions gracefully. Do not ask:

— *Why…?*

— *Why don't you ever…?*

— *Why do you always…?*

"Why" questions tend to put the other person on the defensive.

[1] Cavett Robert, Founder, National Speakers Association

Also avoid accusative, closed-ended questions that result in defensiveness, such as:

— *Did you do that to sabotage me?*

— *Are you out to get me?*

Instead, use a **PowerPhrase to Ask Clarifying Questions,** such as:

- **Help me to understand...**
- **Let me make sure I understand you clearly...**
- **Are you aware...?** (I LOVE this one!)
- **Your intentions are not clear to me. Can you help me out here?**
- **What did you mean by...?**

Power Pointer–Listen With Your Heart

I believe that to understand all is to forgive all. It is easy to find the flaw in other people's thinking. It is harder to find out how it makes sense to them. Listen to learn about them. Listen to understand all. As long as you have judgments, you do not truly understand.

The good news is that you can listen to yourself in the same way. Listen to yourself and others with your heart.

If you are judging yourself or others, think:

- **There is something I do not understand here.**
- **There is a reason that they are behaving this way.**

To know all is to forgive all.

Many of their answers will probably anger or upset you. Consider their words and explore their position more thoroughly before asserting your own. Do not let your reaction stand in the way of managing conflict successfully. Instead, keep listening to them, and continue to

It is easy to find the flaw in other people's thinking. It is harder to find out how it makes sense to them.

seek to understand. Do not say:

— *That is a ridiculous idea!*

— *You are kidding, right?*

— *How could you possibly think that?*

— *You're wrong!*

Instead, use a **PowerPhrase to Acknowledge Without Agreeing**, such as:

- **I see. Tell me more.**
- **This is a big issue for you.**
- **I might feel that way if I was in your shoes.**
- **That's an interesting perspective.**
- **I did not realize that you felt that way.**
- **I had not considered that perspective.**
- **Please continue.**
- **That may be.**
- **I appreciate your sharing your experience. What else do I need to know?**

At various intervals, use **PowerPhrases to Ask Questions That Confirm Understanding**, such as:

- **This is my understanding of what you are saying… What do I still need to know to understand your perspective?**
- **What I hear you saying is… Is my understanding correct?**

Redirect any urge you may have to scream, curse or throw cold water on them, into effective conflict management. Continue to use **PowerPhrases to Ask Clarifying Questions, PowerPhrases to Acknowledge Without Agreeing,** and **PowerPhrases to Ask Questions That Confirm Understanding** until it is clear that you understand them, and they know it. Most people do not make it this far!

Power Pointer–Pick Your Battles

Always be aware of your chances of success when you decide what to address.

Following a merger, my client Donna found herself reporting to a manager who knew far less than she did. The manager decided to relocate the call center to another state because "cost would be less". Donna was more familiar with the numbers than her supervisor was. Donna knew that although wages were lower, cost per dollar ordered was much higher. The decision was already made, so rather than arguing about something that could not be changed, Donna set her focus on what could be affected. She said:

- **You are right that wages are lower there. However, cost per dollar ordered is higher. Let's get some trainers in there to increase their efficiency.**

Pick battles small enough to win and big enough to matter.

Pick battles small enough to win and big enough to matter.

When you listen first, people are much more willing to listen to you.

PowerPhrases to the Rescue

An assistant at one of my seminars named Marcie was the representative of a very difficult client. She said that she had his account because she was the only one who could tolerate him at all. After learning how to make her CASE, Marcie prepared a script to request better treatment from him. She began by saying:

- **I believe that I understand how you want to be treated as my client. May I go through my understanding to make sure it is correct?**

He agreed and she told him of all the things she understood he wanted from her. When the client agreed that her understanding was appropriate, Marcie said:

- **Now I would like five minutes of your time to tell you how I would like to be treated as your representative. Can you offer me that?**

He agreed and she went through her lists of requests. For example, she said:

- **I would like you to view me as someone who is doing what she can to help you.**
- **I want to be able to clarify my understandings.**

When she finished, the client was quiet for several moments. Then he said, "You deserve a raise and a promotion, and I'm going to get you one." He did! He talked to her boss and the result was that she got a raise and a promotion.

When you listen first, people are much more willing to listen to you.

Make Your CASE Step 2: Assert Your Own Position

When the other person agrees that you understand their position, they will be more open to your explanations. Before you speak, you might want to elicit a commitment from them to listen and consider your ideas. Use a **PowerPhrase for Requesting Uninterrupted Time to Express Yourself**, such as:

- **You acknowledge that I understand your position. Will you give me five minutes of uninterrupted time to explain mine?**
- **You have made some valid points that make a lot of sense from where you stand. Please hear me out as I describe how it looks to me.**
- **Are you ready to hear how I see it?**

When the other person agrees that you understand their position, they will be more open to your explanations.

There are three steps to asserting your position in conflict. (A) Describe the problem, (B) communicate the impact, and (C) request a new behavior.

A. Describe the Problem

Open with a description of what happens or what they do in behavioral terms. This means be neutral and leave out all judgment. Think of yourself as an attorney. Attorneys cannot say:

— *You are out to get me.*

— *Obviously, my assignments are of a low priority to you.*

— *You micromanage.*

— *You never respond to me.*

— *I think you were raised in a barn.*

Attorneys must state facts as facts, and leave out opinions (or be subtle about it when do not). You need to speak with the same integrity.

Do not let anyone talk you out of your own experience.

Use **PowerPhrases for Describing the Negative Behavior,** such as:

- **When…**
- **I notice…**
- **The other day…**
- **When I… you…**

Filled in, these sentence stems can sound like the following:

- **When… the time for the meeting regarding the Smith account was changed…**
- **I notice that… the assignment I gave you was moved to the bottom of your project sign-in sheet.**
- **The other day… you checked my work 14 times.**
- **When I spoke… you did not respond.**

Power Thinking to the Rescue

Do you ever doubt your own perceptions when someone disagrees with it? Do not let anyone talk you out of your own experience. Certainly you do want to consider their perspective, but do not let their perspective become more important than your own. Don't think:

— *I must be crazy.*

— *They must be crazy.*

— *I shouldn't be thinking and feeling this way.*

Instead, use Power Thinking, such as:

- **I am the authority on my view of the situation.**
- **They are the authority on their view of the situation.**
- **They have a right to their opinion, and I have a right to mine.**
- **I have a right to express my opinion.**

B. Communicate the Impact

After describing the offending behavior, express the impact, and your thoughts and feelings about it. Do not say:

— *It messes everything up. (Too vague)*

— *I think you don't trust me. (Blaming)*

Instead, use a **PowerPhrase for Expressing the Impact of a Behavior,** such as:

- **What happens is...**
- **The impact is...**
- **I think...**
- **I feel...** (Consider the cautions for "I think" and "I feel" in Chapter 2 before using them.)
- **The effect is...**

Filled in these can sound like:

- **What happens is... I feel alienated from the team.**
- **The impact is... I do not receive my work on time and I do not present well at the meeting.**
- **I think... I'm not trusted.**
- **I feel... uncomfortable.**
- **The effect is... I get confused and make more mistakes.**

Once they understand the impact of their actions tell them what you want them to do.

C. Request a New Behavior

Once the impact is clear, tell them what you want them to do. Do not say:

— *Do this... (Sounds dictatorial)*

— *Don't do that... (Talk about what you WANT, not what you do not want.)*

— *You need to... (Be very careful of sentences that start with you. It can sound controlling.)*

Instead, use a **PowerPhrase for Requesting a New Behavior**, such as:

- **I need…**
- **I want…**
- **What I want to see happen is…**
- **I prefer…**
- **What would work better is…**
- **What needs to happen is…**
- **I need… to be advised of changes as they occur.**
- **I want… us to work out a standard system for prioritizing work.**
- **I prefer… to work on my own, checking in at regularly scheduled intervals.**

Clearly request what new behavior you desire.

Put the above steps together and you get the three-step process for asserting your position.

Three-Step Process for Asserting Your Own Position Without Intensifying the Conflict

Problem	Thoughts/Feelings/ Effect	Request
I sent three inquiries without receiving a response.	I think I am being ignored.	I need a prompt acknowledgement of my inquiries and an indication of when my request will be granted.
My situation is that I have been here for three months and I still do not have a workstation of my own.	I feel frustrated. What happens is I have to carry my materials to wherever I can find a station, and it takes quite a while to sort them out.	My request is that the next time someone leaves, I be given their desk.
When you sell product that were designed for my department…	The effect is that my claims of exclusivity to my clients are invalidated and they lose trust in me.	I need you to stop selling our line. I recommend that you request products to be designed exclusively for your department.
When I speak, I notice you are reading the paper.	I believe that you cannot listen to me and read the paper at the same time.	Please give me your full attention.
The other day you spoke with my staff about turnaround times.	They were upset by the way you addressed them and the standards you expressed.	I suggest we meet and find a solution to this problem together.

Assert your own position without intensifying the conflict.

When you give people corrective feedback, the initial response is usually defensive.

PowerPhrases to the Rescue–Addressing an Impossible Manager

Trainer Carolyn Burke was once a sales manager at a major bank. The Vice President of Sales, Sharon, believed in management by intimidation. Sharon created an atmosphere of fear and paranoia for the people that Carolyn supervised. If they did not meet their sales goals, once a month they were on the phone with Sharon, where she would humiliate them in front of their peers. One day, after finding a woman named Carrie at her desk in tears, Carolyn decided that it was time to address the issue. She scripted out what she planned to say and practiced with her husband.

When she was fully prepared, Carolyn introduced the topic by saying:

- **Sharon, there's an issue I would like to discuss. Can we meet in the conference room?**

Once in the conference room, Carolyn continued by saying:

- **Sharon, the other day I came back to the office and Carrie was at her desk in tears. She had just gotten off the phone with you for not meeting her sales goals and she was very upset.**

Sharon said, — "She should have been. She wasn't doing her job."

Carolyn acknowledged her without agreeing by saying:

- **That may be. May I continue?**
- **I understand the reason why you have these calls is so we will meet our goals and stay off the phone with you. I think you don't know what happens when we get off the phone with you. When we get off the phone with you, we don't**

feel like going out and selling. We are devastated. Our self-esteem is so low, we want to crawl under the desk and hide. Sharon, you know so much. Share what you know with us rather than scaring us. That will increase our commissions, which will increase your commissions as well.

Sharon replied, — "Carolyn Burke, don't you EVER tell me how to do my job again. Get out of here!" Carolyn responded by saying:

- **I understand you're upset. I've just given you feedback. No one enjoys that. I do believe that when you consider what I've told you, you will realize that it will benefit you as well as us.**

Carolyn did not push Sharon to acknowledge what she said at that moment. When we give people corrective feedback, the initial response is usually defensive. Carolyn gave Sharon the information and allowed her time process it. Carolyn's communication was successful. Sharon never made those calls again. Five years later, when Carolyn was leaving the company, Sharon told her that she respected her for addressing the issue that day.

Whether you get acknowledged or not, you reclaim a bit of yourself every time you communicate well.

When you express consequences, it is far better to explain the benefits of cooperating than the costs of non-cooperation.

D. Consequences

Sometimes you will want to include a fourth step for asserting your position—a consequence. When you express consequences, it is far better to explain the benefits of cooperating than the costs of non-cooperation. However, there is a place for both.

Do not say:

— *Do this or else…(Threatening)*

— *If I were you…(Condescending)*

— *You are forcing me to…(Accusatory)*

Instead, use a **PowerPhrase for Explaining Consequences,** such as:

- **This will…**
- **The benefit to you is…**
- **If this happens again, I will…**
- **Next time this happens I will…**
- **What this means for you is…**

Combine one phrase from each category to make a complete and effective statement of your position.

Use a PowerPhrase for explaining consequences

The Four-Step Process to Assert Your Position

Problem	Impact: Thoughts Feelings/Effect	Request	Consequence
I sent three inquiries without receiving a response.	I think I am being ignored.	I need a prompt acknowledgement of my inquiries and an indication of when my request will be granted.	This will keep me from inundating you with repeated requests.
My situation is that I have been here for three months and I still do not have a workstation of my own.	I feel frustrated. What happens is I have to carry my materials to wherever I can find a station, and it takes quite a while to sort them out.	My request is that the next time someone leaves, I be given their desk.	The benefit to you is I will be more efficient in my work.
When you sell product that were designed for my department...	The effect is that my claims of exclusivity to my clients are invalidated and they lose trust in me.	I need you to stop selling our line. I recommend that you request products to be designed exclusively for your department.	If this happens again I will bring the issue to the supervisor.
When I speak, I notice you are reading the paper.	I believe that you cannot listen to me and read the paper at the same time.	Please give me your full attention.	Next time this happens I will wait until I have your full attention to speak.

You can assert your position in one to three steps.

Asserting Your Position in One to Three Steps

While I recommend you decide what you would say for all four steps if you were to use them, sometimes you will want to use shorter statements, omitting some elements.

Problem	Impact: Thoughts/ Feelings/Effect	Request	Consequence
		Please give me your full attention when I speak.	
I have not received a response to the memo I sent last week.			If this continues I will request that you be removed from the project.
		How can I help you get here on time?	
	Clients are threatening to withdraw their accounts.	I need the figures immediately.	

Why not request that you look for solutions together?

In many situations, this will be sufficient. They will say, "sure, no problem", and you will see if your requests are honored. However, sometimes you will either not agree on the problem, or you will not agree on the solution. In that case, move to step 3, and seek solutions.

Make Your Case Step 3: Seeking Solutions

Why not request that you look for solutions together? Use a **PowerPhrase to Request That You Negotiate Solutions Together,** such as:

- **What I want to see happen is for us to negotiate solutions together.**
- **I suggest that we kick around a few ideas to see what solutions we can come up with.**
- **If we could come up with a solution that works for us both, would you be interested?**
- **What would it take to make my request possible?**

- **I believe we can work this out to both of our satisfaction. Will you work with me on this?**
- **I need your help to resolve this.**

Before you can effectively seek solutions, you might need to find a definition of the problem that you both can agree to. In larger issues, it is worth the time to reach a mutual definition of the problem. For example, one of my clients could not get her employee to admit that her actions undermined the team, but she was willing to admit that there was a perception of her not being a team player. They set out to find ways to change the perception. The resulting solutions were effective.

One approach to negotiate solutions is outlined in *How to Deal With Difficult People* by Paul Friedman. It comes from The Federal Mediation and Conciliation Service. It suggests that you both complete the following **PowerPhrases for Seeking Solutions.**

In larger issues, it is worth the time to reach a mutual definition of the problem.

- **I think I should…**
- **You think you should…**
- **I think you should…**
- **You think I should…**

Find the points of agreement, and combine the lists into:

- **We think we should…**

Another powerful way for you to generate options is to brainstorm solutions. You can do it on your own, or you can get with the other parties involved and offer solutions until you get 20 options. Let yourself get a little crazy in your ideas. Tell your mental critic's committee that they will get their turn later. You will welcome logic and common sense during the evaluation phase later.

Once you have evaluated your options, make concrete commitments and arrange follow-up.

Power Pointer–Brainstorming Solutions

At one company where I was doing conflict resolution training, the group decided to brainstorm solutions to see if they could resolve a problem as a group. They chose to brainstorm solutions for conflict in meetings. The meetings were turning into venting sessions. Management was delighted that the group was taking it on themselves to address the problem, because the meetings were a burden to them too.

We thought of solutions until we got twenty. Some were extreme, but we did not evaluate them until later. We narrowed it to five guidelines to implement, which they all agreed on.

They implemented the guidelines and followed up two weeks later to see what they wanted to keep and what to change. Meetings were transformed, but what was really transformed was the group. They learned that they actually wanted the same things and that they could work together to resolve the problem.

Make Your Case Step 4: Evaluating Options and Building Agreements

Once you have at least twenty options on paper, review them and see which ones or one you can agree to. For each option, use **PowerPhrases to Evaluate Options,** such as:

- **Does this option solve the problem?**
- **Can you and I both live with this option?**
- **Is there any way to improve this option?**
- **Is it realistic?**
- **Are you and I both willing to commit to it in writing?**

Once you have evaluated your options, make concrete commitments and arrange follow up. If they resist and say that obviously you do not trust them, say:

- **Putting it in writing ensures we have the same understanding.**
- **My policy is to get agreements as clear as possible to avoid surprises later.**
- **Follow-up enables us to review our decisions in case a situation arises that we did not consider.**

At follow-up, ask:

- **How is it working for you?**
- **What needs to change?**
- **Is there anything we did not anticipate?**

Putting agreements in writing makes the agreement more concrete and creates a higher level of commitment.

Power Pointer–Get it in Writing

Years ago when my son was fourteen, we were negotiating everything in our lives together. I asked what he needed from me and talked about what I needed from him. We had been at odds, but this discussion was framed with an understanding that neither one of us would agree to anything we did not feel good about.

When it came time to put it into a formal agreement in writing, I noticed that my son became much more serious. He was willing to verbally agree to many things that he was not willing to agree to in writing. Putting it in writing made it much more concrete. It creates a higher level of commitment.

Exit Lines

Are you thinking that making your CASE sounds great, but can it be so simple? Of course there are times when they or you get highly emotional and cannot stay calm. Knowing when to stop talking is as important as knowing when to start. If you are upset and emotional, DO NOT CONTINUE! Instead, use an exit line to remove yourself and give yourself time to gain perspective. Do not say:

— *I am out of here…(Too abrupt)*

— *There is no talking to you…(Accusatory)*

— *This is a waste of time… (Negative)*

— *You are an idiot…(Insulting)*

Knowing when to stop talking is as important as knowing when to start.

Instead, use a **PowerPhrase Exit Line,** such as:

- **I need to check on some things before continuing this discussion. Let's meet again at…**
- **I need to take some time to regain perspective before answering you. Let's talk again Friday.**
- **My policy is not to discuss emotionally charged subjects when I am upset. I need some time now. Let's talk later.**
- **You deserve respect. Right now, I'm so angry I can't offer you that. I need ____ minutes.**[2]
- **I'm afraid if we continue this discussion I'll say something I will regret. Let's give it a 24-hour rest.**
- **I value our work relationship too much to speak when I am as upset as I am now. Let's pick this up tomorrow.**
- **I think it is possible that one of us might say something we wish we hadn't. Let's meet later when we are calmer.**

One assistant said that once when she was upset with her boss she said:

[2] Carol Scofield, Conflict Management Skills for Women (videotape) (Mission, KS: SkillPath Publications, 1994).

- **I need to take some time because I'm beginning to forget that you're the boss.**

Use that one at your own risk! While it is clever, it can be taken as aggressive.

Be aware of two important points about using an exit line.

1. Always say when you will be back.
2. After you use the line, you need to LEAVE! Do not say it unless you mean it.

If they follow you and get pushy, say:

- **Now is not a good time.**

Repeat it several times if necessary. You need to make it clear that you do mean what you say. While you are in "time out," review your PowerPhrases and plan how to proceed.

Diffusing Anger

Do not resist anger. Diffuse it instead.

When you assert yourself by giving corrective feedback, a common first response is defensiveness. Expect and allow for that. Do NOT push them to acknowledge anything in that moment if they seem extremely upset.

Have you ever had someone spitting mad around you? Have you had someone who seemed out of control with anger? Do not resist their anger. Diffuse it instead. If they are hurling accusations at you, do not say:

— *That is not true! (Makes them more certain that it is.)*

— *How dare you! (Accusatory.)*

— *Shut up! (Makes them want to talk all the more.)*

Do not say:

— *Calm down! (Invalidates their emotions.)*

— *Be reasonable! (Points out that they are not being reasonable which inflames them more.)*

- — *Can't you see how right I am? (Or anything that they will interpret this way.)*
- — *I do not have to put up with this! (They think you deserve it and are avoiding responsibility.)*

There are six main ways to diffuse anger.(1) Listen, (2) agree, (3) ask specific questions to focus them, (4) humor, (5) stand up to them and (6) go for a solution.

Whatever your goals are, avoid unnecessarily provoking the other person.

PowerPhrases to the Rescue–Choose Words to Diffuse Anger

In her book True Power[3], Linda Larsen gives a dramatic example of using PowerPhrases to diffuse anger. She was abducted by an escaped convict and held at gunpoint for six hours! At one point her abductor took the gun, pointed it straight at her head, cocked the trigger, and asked her "Are you ready to die?" Her mind worked like a computer, searching for the response that would not provoke her agitated captor. Her response was:

- **Well, I suppose if you wanted to kill me there is nothing I can do to stop you.**

He asked, —"Why aren't you on the floor groveling for your life?" To which she replied:

- **Because you have the power.**

What she realized as those words came out of her mouth was that SHE was the one with the power. He was out of control and she was in control. That enabled her to choose responses that helped her to successfully escape. Her goal in that moment was to stay alive. To do that, she needed to align with her captor, not alienate him. Whatever your goals are, avoid unnecessarily provoking the other person. That will enhance your chances of success.

[3] Larsen, Linda, *True Power*, Sarasota FL, Brandywine Publications, 2000

1. Listening to Diffuse Anger

Usually people who are angered expect you to resist. The very act of listening rather than resisting often diffuses anger. When listening to an angry person you will need to use **PowerPhrases to Acknowledge Without Agreeing**, such as:

- **Obviously you feel strongly about this.**
- **I did not know you felt that way.**
- **Tell me more.**
- **What else concerns you?**

Refer back to page 44 for more of these phrases.

People who are angered expect you to resist. The very act of listening rather than resisting often diffuses anger.

Power Listening to the Rescue

Debbie had to fire one of her employees. Unfortunately, this employee's wife, Betty, was on Debbie's management team. Debbie noticed that Betty had become indirectly hostile so she invited Betty to discuss it. The discussion amounted to about twenty minutes of Debby listening to Betty yell, during which Debbie used PowerPhrases to acknowledge her feelings and encourage Betty to speak. After expressing herself this way, Betty seemed relieved, and there was no more indirect aggression.

Months later, there was an opening for a position Debbie wanted in the department Betty oversaw. When Debbie expressed interest she got Betty's full support, and now is very happy in her new position.

Even though Debbie was quite justified in firing Betty's husband and the accusations that were hurled at her were unwarranted, it was in Debbie's interests to resist defending herself and to allow Betty to vent the anger she felt. Do not let your ego tell you to do things that are ultimately not in your best interest.

2. Agreeing to Diffuse Anger

Listen for something you can agree to. It may be that out of a hundred accusations, you can hear only one that has validity. Validate that point! As a skilled conflict manager, listen for truth in everything that is said. There is a good chance that the speaker does not know what the real issue is. Listen for the deeper truth, and help them sort out the issues and move forward into problem solving. A side benefit is that when you validate what truth you find, they often will calm down and be more open to listening.

Listen for truth in everything that is said.

Do not say:

— *Ninety-nine things you said are wrong.*

— *How can you think that?*

— *Aren't you ignoring the following 200 facts?*

Instead, use a **PowerPhrase to Diffuse Anger by Agreeing,** such as:

- **The point you made about ___ hits home.**
- **That may be…**
- **I don't blame you for being upset about…**
- **I hate it when that happens to me too!**
- **I get angry too when…**

Align yourself with them and put yourself in the same boat. While they are attempting to make you the enemy, you see the similarities between you.

Power Thinking to the Rescue

Observe your thoughts when someone is venting anger at you. Don't think:

— *I've got to stop them.*

— *They have their nerve.*

— *I can't handle this!*

Instead, use Power Thoughts, such as:

- **Stay calm.**
- **What can I say to calm them down?**
- **What do they need in this moment?**
- **What is the issue behind their emotion?**
- **What might they be afraid of?**

Choose thoughts that focus on your main goal at that moment–calming them down so that you can focus on the real issue. Do not get caught up in their emotion. You choose your own response.

Diffuse anger by seeking specific information.

3. Ask Specific Questions to Diffuse Anger

Often when people are angry, the accusations are sweeping. You always… you never… you are a such and such. Often they will label you. You can diffuse the anger by seeking specific information to get them to focus on a concrete subject. This tool also keeps you from resisting the accusations.

You will probably have to put yourself on a leash to listen to accusations that are hurled at you in anger! In fact, you will want to deny the accusation even if you don't believe what they are accusing you of is so bad! When they are out of control in anger, this is not the time to say:

— *That's not true.*

— *You're wrong.*

— *How dare you!*

— *Yeah but you…*

Instead, use a **PowerPhrase for Diffusing Anger Through Inquiry,** such as:

- **Exactly what do I say or do that leads you to believe that…**
- **You just said that … (I lied, I am stupid, etc.…) Will you explain what you mean by that?**
- **To really understand your point, I need specific examples.**

This tool usually disarms, as well as forces them to get more logical rather than emotional.

4. Using Humor to Diffuse Anger

The best humor pokes fun at the person using it.

Humor in explosive situations can backfire, so do use these phrases with caution. You do not want to give the impression that you take their concerns lightly. Your goal is to break the angry state and introduce some levity. The best humor pokes fun at the person using it. Avoid humor at the expense of the angry person. Instead, use a **PowerPhrase to Diffuse Anger With Humor,** such as:

- **Someone must have switched stupid pills with my vitamins.**
- **You know, Brad Pitt was saying the exact same thing to me last week!**
- **I wonder if my mother dropped me on my head as a baby!**
- **Don't hurt me! I'm a grandmother!**
- **Is there a mess-up of the month award?**
- **My brain has a mind of it's own sometimes.**
- **Do you smell smoke? I think my brain is burning.**

If these do not sound like PowerPhrases to you, consider this: powerful people are confident enough that they do not need to constantly prove how great they are. In addition, PowerPhrases seek results. The result we seek when someone is out of control is to help him or her calm down so we can proceed to conflict management.

5. Stand Up to an Angry Person

If these PowerPhrases get you nowhere in a situation where someone seems emotionally out of control, you could be communicating with a manipulator or a tester. Some people become deliberately angry to control the listener. Others become deliberately angry to test the listener. Staying calm frustrates the manipulator, and shows them that you are not someone to manipulate. Staying calm proves your strength to the tester. If your attempts to diffuse fail and if you believe that you are dealing with a tester or manipulator, speak up on your own behalf. Do not say:

— *You're manipulating me. (They probably don't realize it.)*

— *Shut up! (Inflames and sounds helpless.)*

Instead, use a **PowerPhrase to Tell an Angry Person How to Treat You,** such as:

- **I care about your problem and when you speak to me in this way, I cannot focus on solutions.**
- **I want to hear what you have to say, and not in this way.**
- **I am here to find resolution. I am not here to be verbally abused. One more comment like that and I will no longer listen.**
- **Are you aware that you are blasting the very person who can help you?**
- **When you speak to me in this way, I do not feel moved to help you.**

The result we seek when someone is out of control is to help him or her calm down so we can proceed to conflict management.

- **I am concerned about your problem and uncomfortable with the way you are expressing it.**
- **Speaking to me in this way is totally unacceptable.**
- **When you are calm, I will be happy to listen to your concerns.**

6. Going for a Solution to Diffuse Anger

Out of control people usually are not ready to talk about solutions until they have had a chance to vent their emotions and assign a bit of blame. Sometimes, however, they will allow you to redirect their attention from the problem on to a solution. Use a **PowerPhrase to Focus on the Solution,** such as:

Out of control people usually are not ready to talk about solutions until they have had a chance to vent their emotions and assign a bit of blame.

- **Let's fix the problem, instead of blame.**
- **What can I do for you now?**
- **How do you see us resolving this problem?**

If they are out of control with anger, use these phrases with caution, as they might become angrier if they have a stronger need to emote than to find resolution.

PowerPhrase to the Rescue–Diffuse Anger by Seeking Solutions

My friend Susan was on a committee that changed the charting for the hospital she worked at. The first day the new charts came into effect, a doctor called and asked,

"Whose crazy idea were these new charts?"

Susan said:

- **I was part of a committee that put these charts together.**

The doctor said, "You nurses are ruining this hospital". To which Susan responded:

- **Sir, there was a doctor on the committee.**

The doctor responded to that by saying, "So now you're blaming the doctors!"

Susan decided that she needed to go for a solution. She said:

- **With things being what they are, what can I do for you now?**

He said "I want the following points documented and on my desk by Monday at ten."

If Susan had tried to show him how irrational his communication was, she would still be arguing with him. Going for a solution sidestepped the fixing of blame.

PowerPhrases for Dealing With Passive-Aggressive Behavior

Passive-aggressive people are out to get you but they use indirect tactics.

Do you find directly angry people easy to deal with compared to the ones who are indirect or passive-aggressive? Passive-aggressive people are out to get you, but they use indirect tactics. If you address the issue directly, they deny the problem, and act innocent.

Passive-aggression comes in four main forms.

1. Mixed messages. ("Not bad for a novice.")

2. Tone of voice conflicts with literal meaning of wording. ("So glad you could make it!" in a sarcastic tone that emphasizes the word "make.")

3. Gestures conflict with words. (Saying "of course" while rolling the eyes.)

4. Actions conflict with words. (Saying, "Let's do it your way!" but not following through.)

People are passive-aggressive for two reasons.

1. They do not know how to or do not feel safe with communicating directly.

2. They can get away with it.

In either case, deal with passive-aggression in a straightforward way. Describe the conflict between what they are saying and what you perceive. Do not say:

— *You lie! (Accusatory)*

— *Oh yeah? Right! (Sarcastic and passive-aggressive)*

Instead, use a **PowerPhrase to Address Passive-Aggressive Behavior Directly,** such as:

Deal with passive-aggression in a straightforward way.

- **Is something bothering you that we need to address? I care about our relationship. If there is something we need to resolve, let's do it.**
- **I am confused because your words say everything is fine, but your tone of voice implies it's not. What's going on?**
- **What do you mean by…?**
- **That remark sounded sarcastic and condescending to me. Did you mean it that way?**
- **When you say ___, this is what I hear… Is that what you mean?**
- **I thought I heard a dig. Did I?**
- **When you said ___, I heard___. That hurts!**

Do not expect them to instantly confess their tactics! Passive-aggressive people will continue the tactics that have worked so well for them until they realize they do not work anymore. If they deny any truth to your perceptions, do not worry about it. If you stay assertive, over time they will stop.

If they accuse you of being too sensitive, you do not need to automatically deny it. Do not say:

— *No, I am not! (Sounds defensive and you are playing their game, not yours.)*

You can simply respond by saying:

- **That may be. If I am sensitive, I think it is important for you to know how your words affect me.**
- **If you believe I am sensitive, why do you make comments like that?**
- **This is not an issue of sensitivity. This is an issue of...**

If they say it was just a joke, you can tell them:

- **If you intended it as a joke, you need to know that I did not find it funny. Instead of being amused, I was hurt.**
- **Sometimes I use humor to mask put-downs or to communicate issues indirectly. If that is what you are doing, and if there is something you need to tell me, please tell me directly.**

Passive-aggressive people will continue their tactics until they realize they do not work anymore.

We always have options of assertiveness.

Power Pointer– It is Hard to See Passive-Aggressiveness in Ourselves.

Georgia was upset that people would criticize coworkers who were not in attendance at meetings. She took the meeting minutes, so one day she took the minutes verbatim. Every dig and every sideswipe went into the minutes. Georgia felt innocent and acted baffled that people were angry about it. Georgia had no idea that her action was passive aggressive. She was being indirectly hurtful. A more assertive approach would have been to say something like:

- **I am uncomfortable when we speak about people behind their backs. I insist that we only talk about people in the same way we would if they were here.**

Of course she would need to be willing to back up her assertion with action. If the behavior continued, she could assert herself again.

- **When we criticize people who are not present, it causes me to believe that you discuss me when I am not here. I find it unacceptable.**

If there is still no response she can walk out of the meeting, asserting:

- **Please invite me back when this discussion has ended.**

Passive-aggressive is hard to see, because we believe that they deserve so much worse than what we are giving them. We always have options of assertiveness.

EXERCISE

I. Listening While Under Attack

Get a friend with whom you feel very comfortable for this exercise, because it will probably stretch your tolerance level! Ask your friend to hurl criticism and accusations at you. If you are really adventurous, tell them the areas you are sensitive about. For example, if being called selfish is a problem for you, tell your friend to call you selfish. If you are not so bold, ask them to limit themselves to specific comments that do not trigger such core issues.

When they make an accusation, respond by telling them what you appreciate about them. Your comments do not have to relate to their criticisms in any way. For example, they might call you selfish, and you respond by saying they have sound business judgment. They say you are stupid and you tell them that they have nice hair.

The purpose of this exercise it to break the pattern on reacting. It is very powerful.

II. Making Your CASE

Problem: Someone expressed your idea to the boss and took credit.

Your Response: You naturally believe you know what happened. The coworker you confided in is not to be trusted! She wronged you! However, do you really know the entire story? Instead of accusing her or getting back at her, you make your CASE! You start by clarifying her position.

What **PowerPhrases to Ask Clarifying Questions** would you use?

1.____

2.____

3.____

She says things that sound like excuses to you, but in order to stay focused on her perspective and to get the entire story, you use a **PowerPhrase to Acknowledge Without Agreeing**. Which ones do you use?

1.____

2.____

3.____

She begins by saying that it was as much her idea as yours. She says she never told the boss it was her idea, he just assumed that it was. She also expressed her own fear about being fired if she did not come up with some great ideas. You are ready to respond, but before you do, you want to verify your understanding by using a **PowerPhrase to Ask Questions That Confirm Understanding**. What do you say?

____

____

Now you know what to say because you understand her position. You want to make certain that she is ready to listen, and you want to set the stage for uninterrupted time. You do this by using a **PowerPhrase for Requesting to Express Yourself Without Interruption.** What do you say?

____

She agrees to hear you out. First, you want to describe the problem using a **PowerPhrase for Describing Negative Behavior.** How do you describe the problem in objective terms?

____

____

Now you want to communicate the impact the behavior had on you by using a **PowerPhrase for Expressing the Impact of a Behavior.** What do you say?

____

____

Next, express your suggested solutions by using a **PowerPhrase for Requesting a New Behavior.** What do you say?

____

____

Congratulations! You asserted your position! However, your coworker responds with sarcasm. She says, "I guess not everyone is as perfect as you are."

You respond by using a **PowerPhrase to Address Passive-Aggressive Behavior Directly.** What do you say?

____

____

Now she knows that you are calm and you are serious. You are ready to reach an agreement. Use a **PowerPhrase for Requesting That You Negotiate Solutions Together.** What do you say?

____

____

She agrees and you come up with several options. What options do you come up with? Be certain there is something to be gained for her as well as you.

____

____

____

____

Together you choose one option. This issue does not seem to call for written agreements or follow up so you skip that step. Thank her for working with you, and decide how much information you feel safe sharing with her in the future.

Chapter 5

PowerPhrases™ for Negotiations to Get You What You Want

Look at the following and say aloud what you see.

OPPORTUNITYNOWHERE

If you saw:
OPPORTUNITY NO WHERE,
you are not alone. If you saw:

OPPORTUNITY NOW HERE,
great job! Your focus was positive!

Your success with negotiations starts with picturing a positive outcome. Jim Cathcart said, "The hardest part about getting where I am today was picturing myself being where I am today."[4] Similarly, the hardest part about having a successful negotiation is in being able to picture the possibility. The second hardest part is to know what to say. That's where PowerPhrases are so handy! PowerPhrases will serve you from pre-negotiation to post-negotiation.

The hardest part about having a successful negotiation is in being able to picture the possibility.

Pre-negotiation Essentials
Research Before Beginning to Negotiate

Most of your work in a negotiation takes place before you sit at the negotiation table. Doing your homework can take time, but it is time invested, not spent. PowerPhrases can help.

[4] Jim Cathcart, The Pros Speak About Success, (Mission KS: SkillPath Publications, 1999)

Before you embark on your negotiation, find out:

1. What are the standards in the area, and what is a reasonable range?
2. What do you want, and what are you willing to accept?
3. What are they likely to want and why?
4. What are your deadlines as well as theirs?
5. What are their options if you cannot come to agreement and what alternatives do you have? (This is called walk-away power.)

As part of your research, talk to:

1. People who have already negotiated with the person or organization you will be negotiating with.
2. People who work with the person or team you will be negotiating with. For example, the design department can provide you with useful information about the sales department.
3. Neighbors or neighboring business people.
4. The person you will be negotiating with.

Doing your homework can take time, but it is time invested, not spent. PowerPhrases can help.

Use **PowerPhrases to Get Information About the Other Person's Situation,** such as:

- **What pressures are they under?**
- **What deadlines are they under?**
- **What is the mood in the organization right now?**
- **What kind of arrangements have they made with others either currently or in the past?**
- **If I offered ____, would I be in the ballpark?** (This one is for a disinterested party only. It will sound like an offer if you use it as a probe with the negotiator.)
- **What alternatives do they have to making a deal with me?**
- **How willing are they to take a risk in this matter?**
- **To whom does the negotiator answer?**

- **Why do they want what they do? What need are they trying to meet?**
- **How flexible are they?**
- **How do they decide...?**

Prepare yourself as much as you can before you actually begin a negotiation. While you certainly will be uncovering information in the actual negotiations process, get as much information as you can before you approach the table.

Setting the Tone

Once you believe you have learned all that you can, initiate the negotiation in a way that creates an atmosphere of confidence, ease and mutual gain. Use words that suggest benefit to the other person. You may choose to avoid the word "negotiate," which can imply a winner and a loser. Don't say:

Initiate the negotiation in a way that creates an atmosphere of confidence, ease and mutual gain.

— *Let's negotiate.*

— *I'll do whatever it takes to win your business.*

— *I'll have you seeing things my way in no time.*

Instead, use a **PowerPhrase to Initiate a Negotiation,** such as:

- **If we could work out a plan that benefits us both, would you be interested?**
- **Let's come to an agreement on this.**
- **Let's work together to find a plan that works for both of us.**
- **I am here to work with you.**
- **Let's discuss the situation and come up with a solution we both are happy with. I do not want either of us to agree to anything that does not satisfy both our needs.**
- **We have a challenge. Let's find a solution together.**

- **I'm convinced that we can find an agreement that we both like.**
- **I have an idea I want to share with you. I need 15 minutes of your undivided attention. Would 3:00 this afternoon work?**

If the tone of a negotiation is not favorable for solutions, focus on lightening the tone before you dive into the negotiation details.

Power Pointer–Set the Tone Immediately

I was called in to assist a national company with management-employee negotiations. The manager who introduced me was light and playful with the group until we were ready to begin. At that point he introduced me by telling the group how serious things were and warning them of how they needed to listen, not interrupt, do what I said and shape up. He sounded condescending and patronizing. Everyone's faces fell as a me-against-you atmosphere was created. I knew that if I was going to win any trust from the employees, I needed to change that perception fast. I also needed to avoid offending the manager who had called me in. I said:

- **Michael is right. This is a serious situation and it does need to be taken seriously. Because it is so serious, we need to relax and have as much fun as we can as we go about resolving the issues that face us today. Serious solutions to serious issues come from a state of openness and relaxation. That is when we are our most creative, and that is how we will find answers that satisfy both sides here.**

The tone changed back to one of lightness, cooperativeness and one where solutions could be uncovered.

If the tone of a negotiation is not favorable for solutions, focus on lightening the tone before you dive into the negotiation details.

To help create a relaxed attitude, personalize the conversation. Use their name, and make it a conversation between two people, not two positions. Don't say:

– *ABC Widgets has a proposal they would like to make to XYZ What's It's.*

Instead, use a **PowerPhrase to Personalize the Negotiation,** such as:

- **Kathy, I would like to discuss the deal I can offer you.**
- **Bill, sit down and get comfortable before we begin.**
- **Matt, I hear that you are a skilled negotiator.**
- **Janet, it is obvious that you are very experienced in this area.**

Always be certain that you are negotiating with the person who has the authority to make a deal. You can find that out with **PowerPhrases to Find the Decision Maker**, such as:

- **Who else would you need to consult before we can come to final terms?**
- **If we reach an agreement, will anyone else have to approve?**
- **How does it work around here? Can an individual such as yourself make this decision?**
- **If we reach an agreement today, can we move ahead?**
- **If we came to an agreement here today, what would your next step be?**
- **If we strike a deal, can you approve it?**
- **Is there someone else involved in this deal with you?**
- **If you are happy with what we conclude here, when can we get started?**

If someone else does need to be consulted, either say:

To help to create a relaxed attitude, personalize the conversation.

- **I am unwilling to negotiate without the decision maker present.**

Or say:

- **I would be happy to sit in on meetings with the final decision maker to provide backup information.**

Be aware that if the person you are negotiating with is not the final authority, you might give them enough information to be convinced themselves, but not enough for them to convince someone else. Also, many times when a deal is submitted to a "higher authority" for approval, they are using a tactic to come back with a better deal for them.

Many times when a deal is submitted to a "higher authority" for approval, they are using a tactic to come back with a better deal for them.

Graciously Asking Probing Questions

Once the tone is set, you are negotiating with the right person, and you are ready to begin discussing issues, put the initial focus on them and their needs.

Use a **PowerPhrase to Solicit Their Position**, such as:

- **What goals do you have for today?**
- **How would you like to see this discussion turn out?**
- **Is there anything you want me to know?**
- **What do you see as our common ground here?**
- **Tell me what you want from me/us.**
- **I want to make certain this turns out in a way that works for everybody. How do you see that happening?**
- **How will you know…(which is the supplier you want)?**

Listen, listen, and listen to what they have to say. You will do your best negotiating when you do far more listening than talking! Ask clarifying questions, acknowledge without agreeing, and learn everything that you can.

Use a **PowerPhrase to Ask Clarifying Questions in Negotiations**, such as:

- **Could you expand on that?**
- **Please give me more details about…**
- **I need more precise information about that last point.**
- **Is there anything else we need to discuss that would add significant cost to us?**
- **Have I summarized everything?**

Paraphrase their offers back to them, using a **PowerPhrase to Clarify Understanding**, such as:

- **Am I correct in understanding that…?**
- **I think I understand what you are saying, but I want to be certain I know just what you mean. Are you saying that…?**
- **What I understand you to be saying is…**
- **Let me check to see if I understand you correctly. Are you saying that…?**

Be certain your understanding of their position is accurate before you assert your own.

You will do your best negotiating when you do far more listening than talking!

Power Pointer–The Importance of Acknowledgement

When I coach people during negotiations, I always look for the areas where the parties are in need of acknowledgement. In one discussion, Joe was pointing out to Susan the ways in which she was not giving as much as he expected of her. Susan became defensive and insisted that she was bending over backwards to meet his expectations. Susan was unable to hear how she was falling short because she was seeking acknowledgement of the effort she was putting forward. Joe was unwilling to acknowledge her efforts because he expected more. He was concerned that if he acknowledged her, she would not continue to improve. This is a common impasse. When I was able to get them to see the nature of their stalemate they both relented and were able to give the other the needed acknowledgement and move on. Many times, an unmet need for acknowledgement is the greatest obstacle to finding solutions. People want to get credit for whatever they give.

Look for the areas where the parties are in need of acknowledgement.

Maintaining Early Neutrality

Do you ever have an emotional reaction to the other person's offer? No matter how unreasonable or exciting their offer seems to you in the beginning, maintain a sense of neutrality early in the negotiation. Get a complete picture before you respond to the pieces. Your previous homework of determining standards and alternatives will give you power in responding to their offers. If you do not have attractive options or if their initial offer is very reasonable, you might be tempted to show enthusiasm that could weaken the possibilities of getting concessions. Even if you feel your very survival depends on working out a deal, don't say:

— *I've got to have this or I'll die!*

— *This is exactly what I've been looking for!*

— *That's a terrific buy!*

— *You are our only supplier.*

Instead, use a **PowerPhrase to Sound Calm in Negotiation**, such as:

- **I think we might be able to work out a deal.**
- **What you have could work for me.**
- **Let's talk specifics and see if there is a way we can make this work.**

Early neutrality keeps your options open.

Early neutrality keeps your options open.

Making Your Offer

When you are ready to make an offer, state your needs and offers clearly and confidently. Don't say:

— *I really don't like asking you to do this but…*

— *I was hoping that maybe you possibly could…*

— *You probably won't want to, but…*

Use a **PowerPhrase for Making an Offer**, such as:

- **I propose that…**
- **In my view, a fair solution would be…**
- **I strongly recommend that…**
- **One solution that might work for us both is…**
- **One fair arrangement would be…**
- **If we do ____, it would benefit you by___.**

Use specific amounts. Don't say:

— *I'll give you around $3000.*

Instead, use a **PowerPhrase for Stating a Specific Amount**, such as:

- **I am prepared to offer $2973.**

- **I will have this completed by June 13 at 3:30 PM.**

The other party will be less likely to argue with a specific amount or deadline. State your needs clearly. Without being frivolous, ask for what you really want, not just what you think you can get.

- **What I want is___. What this would mean to you is...**
- **What I want is___ by ___ because___.**

Then show how you are able to fill their needs. Be sure to emphasize why it is a great deal for them.

Use **PowerPhrases to Communicate Value to Them,** such as:

- **What this means for you is...**
- **I can help you by...**
- **Obviously ____ is important to you. I can help you with...**
- **One of the advantages I/we offer is...**

The other party will be less likely to argue with a specific amount or deadline.

Power Thinking to the Rescue–Starting High Can Benefit Them as Well as You

When you ask for what you really want rather than being limited by what you think you can get, you are much more likely to end up better off. If your initial position is high but not frivolous, they have more room to talk you down and still give you a good deal. Imagine your initial offer is $15, but you come down to $10. They can go back to their boss and say they got you down 33%!

Now, imagine you start at $12, and go down to $9. When they report the results they do not look as good, even though the price is more favorable!

Don't think:

— *They might think I'm trying to take advantage of them.*

— *They might get upset if I ask for what I really want.*

Instead, think:

- **The worst that can happen is that they will say no.**
- **This is what I want and this is what it's worth, so this is what I will ask for.**
- **I need to create some room for them to work with.**

If you have areas of weakness, minimize the impact by addressing them directly.

If you have areas of weakness, minimize the impact by addressing them directly.

Use a **PowerPhrase to Minimize Weakness**, such as:

- **Although we do not have the experience you normally require, what we do offer is...**
- **What we offer instead of...is...**
- **It is true that ___ is not our strong point, however, it is a minor issue in this discussion.**

Then move on to emphasize the parts of the deal that they like.

Get feedback from them regarding your offer by using a **PowerPhrase to Solicit Feedback for Your Offers**, such as:

- **What do you think of this idea?**
- **Do you have any concerns with this proposal?**
- **What do you like about my offer?**

If their expectations are unrealistic, let them know without offending. Don't say:

— *It's not fair.*

— *You're way off base.*

Instead, use a **PowerPhrase to Suggest the Range**, such as:

- **Your offer is not competitive.**
- **I cannot come close to that.**
- **Those expectations are unrealistic.**
- **My budget is not close to your range.**

If they do not respond immediately, remain silent until they do.

Give and Take in Negotiations

If their initial offer is ridiculously low or ridiculously high, consider not countering.

If their initial offer is ridiculously low or ridiculously high, don't say:

— *Oh no! This is going to cost me more than I thought!*

— *You're crazy!*

— *That's highway robbery!*

— *What is your problem?*

— *I disagree.*

Instead, consider not countering. Be prepared with **PowerPhrase Responses to Their Offers.** Say:

- **That's an interesting offer.**
- **Let's get serious.**
- **I'm confused.** (Silence).
- **I can begin to negotiate seriously with you when you recommend ideas that are reasonable.**
- **I believe you want to be fair with me, but this offer is not reasonable.**
- **That offer tells me that you are not serious about coming to an agreement. Am I right?**

Power Pointer–Life IS a Negotiation

When Sandy began negotiations for a divorce settlement, she did not realize that she was in a negotiation. She suggested settlements that seemed fair to her. Her husband was playing the negotiation game in a very different way. He began with an extreme position that was in many ways unreasonable.

Because Sandy did not consider this to be a negotiation, she was not prepared for her husband's approach. As a result, her very fair position became the starting point for her position in the negotiation. Her husband was pushing her toward a final settlement that was a middle ground between her position and her husband's extreme position–an outcome that favored him.

When Sandy woke up to what was really going on, she began to push for concessions she never believed she could get. She was shocked when her husband responded by relenting on some other things that she did not expect.

If you limit yourself to what you think you can get, you relinquish much of your power.

Be aware of the other party's attitude. Be aware that some negotiators do not respect soft negotiators and actually prefer to work with people who pursue stronger positions. They enjoy the game, as well as the sense of victory that comes with overcoming some of the demands of a tough "opponent."

Consider countering an extreme offer with a counter proposal that is equally extreme.

Alternatively, you can counter with your own extreme offer.

- **If that is your initial offer, my initial offer will have to be as extreme in the other direction.**

Or you can ask:

- **Where did you get that figure?**
- **What caused you to decide on that…(price, deadline, specification)?**
- **If you were in my seat would you consider that a serious offer?**

Do not wait for the fear to go away. Take action anyway.

Power Pointer–Speaking Powerfully Can Take Getting Used To!

One of my clients was very uncomfortable after reading this book. Fred was in the middle of a negotiation to sell a business. Fred's habit was to give in, go along with what the other person wanted, and "jump through hoops" to meet someone else's demands. The only alternative he saw was to be combative. Fred wanted to respond in a different way and the idea frightened him.

We found the middle ground of being open, firm and committed to a fair deal. We worked out the PowerPhrases to back him up in his new stance.

Fred found that having the words gave him the courage to be his own advocate. The words did not eliminate his fear, however. Despite his fear he was able to stand his ground and speaking was easier for him the next time. Do not wait for the fear to go away. Be prepared with your PowerPhrases, and forge ahead!

Even when offers are within range or better than you imagined, usually you will want to go after a sweeter deal, if only to make them feel good about the deal they make. When you accept an offer too quickly, they will think that they went too cheap. If it is a reasonable offer, affirm that with a **PowerPhrase to Express Partial**

Disagreement, such as:

- **Your offer is reasonable for the most part. There are some areas that concern me…**
- **While I agree on the whole, I have trouble agreeing with the point about…**

You can counter their offer by using a **PowerPhrase to Counter an Offer**, such as:

- **I can offer you ___, if you can give me___.**
- **I understand you feel your price is justified. However, I can only pay…**
- **I need… because…**
- **That's not what I had in mind.**
- **I need you to do better than that.**
- **The best I can do is…**
- **Is that the best you can do?**
- **What is your bottom line?**
- **What would it take to get you to raise (lower) your price?**
- **What if we changed (specifications) (deadline) (the price)?**
- **I was thinking more along the lines of …**
- **Would you consider…?**
- **What would you say to…?**
- **Let's brainstorm options together.**

If they need to think about it, offer to be part of their thinking process.

Next, start the brainstorming process.

Brainstorming

You have an infinite number of possible ways to design a deal. Use brainstorming to generate as many ideas as possible in order to come up with creative solutions. Start by thinking of as many ideas as you can without worrying about why any of them will not work.

When you want to brainstorm with the other person, use a **PowerPhrase to Initiate the Brainstorming Process**, such as:

- **I've run out of ideas. How do you think we can resolve this?**
- **What do you REALLY want?**
- **What's the craziest solution you can think of to this problem?**
- **How can we expand on the ideas we already have on the table?**
- **Suppose we were to…**
- **What if…**
- **Let's assume…**

When you brainstorm, remember that there are no bad or ridiculous ideas. A "crazy idea" can lead to a great one. Evaluate ideas separately from creating them.

You have an infinite number of possible ways to design a deal.

If some of the ideas are negative, translate them into positives. If you consider suggesting:

— *I can refuse to fill orders that are under 30 days.*

Say:

- **I can fill orders that are over 30 days.**

Suspend judgment while you brainstorm, and evaluate these ideas later.

Brainstorming together works best when the trust level is high. The best deals are made when you both are helping each other meet your goals. Of course, ultimately you both will be loyal to your self or organization. Be alert for objections and tactics.

Dealing With Objections and Tactics

Be prepared for objections and tactics as well as the objections that are used as tactics. When they state an objection, use a **PowerPhrase to Overcome**

Objections, such as:

- **I understand how you feel. Many others have felt the same way. What they found was ___.**
- **Are you saying that if I can satisfy this objection, we would have a deal?**
- **Is that the only barrier between you and an agreement?**
- **It's because I know that you are concerned with (their objection) that I think this is a fabulous offer for you.**
- **What makes you say that?**
- **What's keeping you from getting the best?**

Need to Think About It

If they say that they need to think about it, respectfully offer to be a part of their thinking process, so that they won't talk themselves out of it due to lack of understanding.

The brainstorming process works best when the trust level is high.

Use a **PowerPhrase to Counter Their Need to Think About It**, such as:

- **What questions remain?**
- **Could you think about it out loud?**
- **I can help you to think about it if you will tell me what your concerns are.**

Offer your support as a service to them in helping to clarify their concerns.

Split the Difference

If they want to split the difference and they are within range, use a **PowerPhrase to Raise the Range**, such as:

- **I'm at (ten) and you're at (six). Are you suggesting that you could come up to (eight)? Let me discuss that with my people and let you know.**

The range is now between eight and ten. This makes nine seem reasonable.

If they want to split the difference and they are out of range, make value the criteria.

Use a **PowerPhrase to Focus the Discussion on Value**, such as:

- **You are offering me ___. What standard did you use to get that amount?**
- **I would gladly split the difference if I thought that doing so would result in a fair amount. In this case I do not find it reasonable.**

Splitting the difference can be an attempt to frame the figures in a way that might not be relevant.

Nibblers

Never make a concession without receiving something of value in return.

Never make a concession without receiving something of value in return. If they are "nibbling"–meaning that they are asking for many seemingly insignificant concessions–and the concessions are adding up, use a **PowerPhrase to End Nibbling Negotiators**, such as:

- **If I do that for you, what will you do for me?**
- **If you have to have that, I have to have this.**

Even if what you ask for is relatively insignificant, it makes it clear that you are setting boundaries.

Good Guy-Bad Guy

If you haven't run into the good guy-bad guy game, you have at least seen it on television. This can happen when you are negotiating with a team. One negotiator is "on your side" and the other is the "bad" one. The "good" one tries to convince you to trust them to help you to deal with the "unreasonable" one. Challenge them on it.

Use a **PowerPhrase to Challenge the Good Guy-Bad**

Guy Game, such as:

- **You aren't going to play good guy-bad guy with me, are you?**
- **I think ___ is playing bad guy, but let's not approach it that way. Let's take the win-win approach.**

Deal with indirect behavior in negotiations the same way you do in conflict. Let them know you see through their game.

Bogey

A bogey is when the other person claims to be powerless due to a limited budget, deadlines, quality standards, etcetera. Test it out.

Use a **PowerPhrase to Test a Constraint**, such as:

- **If I found the perfect item for (20%) more, should I bother showing it to you?**
- **Who has the authority to (exceed the budget, change the deadline, alter specifications)?**
- **Have there been situations where you have exceeded the budget? How can we make this situation like that one?**

Deal with indirect behavior in negotiations directly.

Use these PowerPhrases to find the limits to their stated constraints.

Use Some Tactics of Your Own

A. Higher Authority

You can try to get a more favorable agreement by referring to a higher authority. If they ask for a concession you do not wish to give, use a **PowerPhrase to Defer to a Higher Authority**, such as:

- **I can agree to x, but beyond that I will have to consult my general manager, who is out of town for the next two weeks.**

- **Our policy is…**
- **I can't sell this to my manager.**

Many times they will concede rather than wait.

B. Last Minute Concessions

You also can ask for some last minute concessions by using a **PowerPhrase for Extracting Last Minute Concessions,** such as:

- **You've got a deal if you will…**
- **I'll do it if you'll…**

Often at that point, they are so ready to firm up the deal that they will give away new concessions.

Know When and How to Walk Away

If you are willing to walk away from a deal, that willingness gives you power.

If you are willing to walk away from a deal, that willingness gives you power. If you discover and create options before beginning the negotiation, you will not settle for less than you deserve.

When you tell them you are ready to walk away, don't say:

— *Take it or leave it.*

— *Accept my offer or I'm outta here.*

Instead, use a **PowerPhrase for Rejecting an Offer,** such as:

- **I find your offer unacceptable.**
- **No, your offer does not work for me.**
- **If that is the best you can do, we might as well not waste any more of each other's time.**
- **Perhaps we will be able to find mutually acceptable terms in future negotiations.**

Do not give an ultimatum unless you are serious about it.

Sealing the Deal

When things are lining up the way you like them, be sure to confirm the deal. Don't say:

– *Think about it and get back to me.*

– *You don't want this, do you?*

Instead, use a **PowerPhrase to Ask for an Agreement,** such as:

- **This makes sense. Let's go ahead and make it happen.**
- **When shall we start?**
- **I believe we have a fair solution. Let's get the paperwork started and have it ready by ___.**
- **What will it take to get a commitment from you now?**
- **Shall we put that in writing?**

Be sure to confirm the deal.

Power Pointer–Get it in Writing!

I was coaching Bill through the sale of a franchise. He had sold it three years prior, and the man who bought it walked out on the business and turned it back to Bill without any notice. The last thing Bill wanted to do was come out of retirement, so he was very anxious to find a buyer.

He was lucky to find a buyer very quickly, and they worked as a team to keep the business going while negotiation details were being handled. The ownership of the franchise was transferred, they worked furiously to build up the inventory, and it looked like a smooth transition.

Bill was very happy about the feeling of good will in how it all unfolded, and because he had known the buyer for years, he was comfortable with acting on a verbal agreement of terms and the understanding that they would use the previous buyer's contract. Despite my misgivings, he was not in a hurry to get the contract in writing. He was very shocked when he received the contract. It included a clause that said "if payments are made on time for nine years, the tenth year is forgiven". That amounted to a 10% reduction in fee.

At this point he has lost all negotiation power and ended up agreeing to a deal that he did not like.

No matter how good it all feels, get it in writing as soon as you can.

No matter how good it all feels, get it in writing as soon as you can.

If you cannot get them to commit on the spot, get them to commit to your next communication. Rather than leaving the discussion open, use a **PowerPhrase to Assure a Follow-Up Commitment**, such as:

- **When will you have your decision? Let's meet that**

day at ___ and wrap this up.

If they say they will call you, ask when you can expect to hear from them. Once they have told you, use a **PowerPhrase for Maintaining Control of the Follow-up,** such as:

- **If I haven't heard from you by ___ I will call you.**

Acknowledging Their Decision

Always be sure to acknowledge them for having made a good deal. Don't say:

— *I scored!*

— *If you were a better negotiator, you could have gotten more. (It happens!)*

Instead, use a **PowerPhrase for Acknowledging Their Decision**, such as:

- **You will be delighted with…**
- **I believe you did well for yourself.**
- **You are obviously skilled at negotiating.**

Now celebrate the fact that YOU are skilled at negotiating!

Always be sure to acknowledge them for having made a good deal.

EXERCISE

Imagine you want your boss to purchase a new piece of equipment for you, such as a printer or copy machine. What information do you want to obtain before initiating the negotiation?

____

____

____

Some of this information will be obtained from other people. What PowerPhrases will you use to request it?

____

____

____

Before you address the issue with your boss, you need to be clear about what you want and why. List your position (what you are asking for) below, followed by your reason for wanting what you do.

Your position:

____

____

____

Reason for wanting what you do:

____

____

____

What do you anticipate your boss's position will be, and why?

Boss's position:

____

____

____

Reason for boss's position:

____

____

Let's say you want this piece of equipment because you are frustrated by the inconvenience of using group equipment. However, you present your desire in terms of the benefit to the boss. What PowerPhrases do you use?

____

____

The boss says she will review your recommendations and get back to you. What PowerPhrases will you use to maintain control of the follow-up?

____

____

____

Quiz

When is most of the work done in a negotiation?

____

What PowerPhrases can you use at that stage?

____

____

What do you have when you take the "n" off of negotiation?

____

Which PowerPhrases address the ego of the other party in negotiation?

____

____

In a negotiation, who is likely to be the most persuasive—the one who talks the most, or the one who talks the least?

____

____

Exercise

Tape record a conversation when you are talking to a friend about something that they know a lot about and you know very little and you want to learn more. Play it back and evaluate who spoke the most.

Next record yourself trying to persuade them of something. Play it back and see who did the most talking.

If you were being truly persuasive, you would have done as little talking and as much listening as you did in the first part of the exercise. In order to be truly persuasive, ask questions and listen! PowerPhrases say it in as few words as possible. That gives you lots of time to listen!

CHAPTER 6:

PowerPhrases™ That Sell

Selling... negotiating... what is the difference? Selling creates acceptance of an idea, and negotiating spells out the terms. Certainly the two concepts do overlap. Yet, there is enough difference that I am making the chapters separate.

Although this chapter is geared toward the professional sales person, if you do not have sales as part of your title, please study this chapter anyway! The PowerPhrases in this chapter will enable you to be more persuasive in life no matter what your focus is. Use the **PowerPhrases for Getting an Appointment** to get your boss to discuss your latest inspiration. Use the **PowerPhrases to Determine Needs** to find out whether the mechanic would be open to accepting frequent-flier miles instead of cash. Use the **PowerPhrases to Create Value** to show your boss that it would benefit her for you to get a copy machine of your own. Use the **PowerPhrases for Obtaining Commitment** to extract a promise from your spouse to take you to Hawaii. Just as we are all constantly negotiating, we are all constantly selling things and ideas. We might as well master the PowerPhrases to do it effectively.

Selling creates acceptance of an idea, and negotiating spells out the terms.

Know Your Objectives at Every Point of the Sale

Remember that PowerPhrases are clear about the results

they want to obtain with each expression. At different stages, you will have significantly different goals. When you are seeking an appointment, you must remember that your goal at that time is to get the appointment, NOT to close the sale. When you are investigating the needs of the prospect, your goal at that time is to discover the needs of the prospect, it is NOT to close the sale at that time. The PowerPhrases are specific to the immediate goal they serve.

Getting the Appointment in Cold Calls

The first step in getting an appointment is to get the attention of the prospect. The technique is simple!

Use the strongest **PowerPhrase to Get a Prospect's Attention** that exists. Call them by their name.

- **Hello, Mr./Mrs./Ms. ____.**

PowerPhrases are specific to the immediate goal they serve.

Then identify yourself.

- **This is ___ from ___.**

Next, briefly describe the purpose of your call. One approach would be to use a **PowerPhrase to Create Interest in What You Are Selling**, such as:

- **If you believed that I could help you to meet your goals, you would want to hear about it, wouldn't you?**
- **I'm calling to show you a better way of doing business.**
- **Have you considered that your business could benefit from using ___?**
- **I can show you how you can add to your business by___.**
- **In x minutes, I can show you how our product can save your business $___. Can you give me those minutes?**

- **In a few minutes I can show you how to increase your bottom line by ___.**
- **I have something your company needs.**
- **How important is it to increase your bottom line?**
- **I represent a product that will make your life easier.**

Another approach is to use a **PowerPhrase to Allude to a Referral,** such as:

- **___ suggested I call you. I have done a lot of work for her, and she suggested we might be of service to you.**
- **I'm calling because ___, who has been a client of mine since ___, is delighted with the results and felt certain that you would want to consider what we offer. Was he right?**

Next you want to get a dialogue going by using a **PowerPhrase to Open a Discussion by Asking Questions They Can Answer Yes To,** such as:

When you ask questions they can say yes to, you get them in a "yes" thinking style.

- **Is saving money important to you?**
- **Would you like to know how to increase motivation in your staff?**
- **Could you use an extra hour in the day?**
- **Does increased productivity interest you?**
- **We've been helping companies like yours prosper in today's marketplace. Would you like to know how?**
- **Do you ever get the sense that things take much longer than they should?**

When you ask questions they can say yes to, you get them in a "yes" thinking style. Remember, at this point your goal is to get an appointment where you can provide them with complete information. Get them saying yes, and when you request the appointment, they will already be on a yes track. Explain how you can address

When they offer an objection, repeat the objection back to them.

their problem, but give only enough information to sell the appointment. Then ask for the appointment clearly. Don't say:

– *Could we meet?*

– *Can you fit me in sometime?*

– *I'll be in the neighborhood anyway next week and I'd like to stop by.*

Instead, use a **PowerPhrase to Get an Appointment**, such as:

- **Let's meet and discuss this in detail. Does Tuesday at 3:00 work for you?**
- **I suggest we talk in person Wednesday at 2:45. Can we plan on that?**
- **It will be more efficient and save us time if we talk face to face. I suggest we meet this Friday at 1:00.**
- **Can you free up 15 minutes to meet with me on Monday, or would Tuesday be better?**
- **Let me come by to explore and explain exactly what I can do for you.**

Sometimes getting the appointment will be that simple and sometimes it won't. When they offer an objection, repeat the objection back to them.

Follow with a **PowerPhrase to Overcome Their Objections to Meeting With You**. If they say they are too busy, say:

- **Is it as hectic there as it is here? I'm busy too, and that is why I do not want to waste either of our time. I am convinced that the time will be well spent.**
- **I had someone else tell me that just a few days ago. After meeting with me for 15 minutes, she was glad she made the time. May I tell you what she discovered while meeting with me?**
- **Is having too much to do with too little time your**

biggest challenge right now? I can reclaim hours each week for you.

- **My goal is to eliminate your time pressures with what my product offers.**
- **Can you find a few minutes to learn how to save time?**
- **That's exactly why we should get together!**
- **That's why I work very hard at making my presentation as brief as possible.**

> ***Power Pointer–Be Pleasantly Persistent.***
>
> *It can be a trick to know the difference between persistence and being pushy. Have you ever had someone overcome your resistance to meeting with him or her and been glad they did? The difference is usually in whether the salesperson is service oriented or not. Before you persist, ask yourself--"Do I believe that it is in THEIR interest to meet with me?" If the answer is yes, then proceed with confidence that you are serving their interest.*

Most sales happen after the fifth attempt!

If they request literature, say:

- **I don't send out literature, however, I can do better than that. I can meet with you personally…**
- **It would take you longer to read any information I could send you than it would for me to explain it. If time is important, let's meet face-to-face.**

If they say they are not interested, do you immediately back down and give up? Most sales happen after the fifth attempt! Most people quit after the first attempt. Ten percent of sales people ask five times and get eighty percent of the yes'es. You may decide that this person is not a true prospect, but if you believe that they need what

If you believe that they need what you have to offer, keep asking.

you have to offer, keep asking. Say:

- **Many of my loyal customers initially say just that, until they understand the nature of the product I represent.**
- **Really? You are concerned with the well being of the company, aren't you?**
- **Do you mind telling me what you are interested in? Saving money? Improving morale?**
- **I must not have communicated what I offer very well, because I believe if I did, you would be interested.**
- **I don't expect that you would be interested until you saw how my service can improve performance.**
- **That surprises me. Can you explain why?**
- **You must have a good reason to say that. Can you explain it to me please?**

If you believe that they are a true prospect, keep referring back to the **PowerPhrases to Get an Appointment** until you are convinced that this is a dead end or you have an appointment.

Establishing Wants and Needs at the Appointment

A. Situation Questions

While you will probe somewhat during the initial call to uncover wants and needs, most of this takes place face-to-face. Do not make the mistake of many sales professionals who move too quickly from the exploration stage into describing features and benefits of what they offer. People need to become aware of their problem and to feel the extent of its impact before they have much interest in hearing how you can solve that problem.

While you will want to get background information

about the company from your prospect, questions that can be answered through preparatory research will not impress anyone, and those questions are not PowerPhrases. Do not sound like an interviewer. Don't ask:

— *What do you produce?*

— *What are they composed of?*

— *How long have you been in business?*

— *How many people work here?*

or similar questions that you could research elsewhere. Particularly, do not ask questions that are unrelated to what the buyer is saying. Tie questions into what the buyer is saying and what the buyer's concerns are.

Use a **PowerPhrase to Determine the Situation of the Buyer,** such as:

- **Many of our customers have been affected by ___. How has that impacted you?**
- **How are you responding to (the recent change in market regulations)?**
- **How did you decide (to purchase the system that you are using now)?**

Questions that can be answered through preparatory research will not impress anyone.

Consider your sales presentation as prime real estate. Whatever you build there must pay for itself in added value. Situation questions are PowerPhrases only when the information cannot be obtained prior to the sales interview.

B. Questions to Uncover Problems

Your questions about their concerns and difficulties will give you more value than situation questions. Ask questions about the challenges their situation creates.

Use **PowerPhrases to Uncover Problems,** such as:

- **Is (turnover) a problem here?**

- **Do (delayed deliveries) ever cost you business?**
- **What challenges do you have with (quality control)?**
- **How often are (deliveries delayed)?**
- **Is there an area where (quality control) could be improved?**
- **How satisfied are you with (your current supplier)?**
- **Are you concerned about (upcoming technology changes)?**
- **Where does (the process tend to break down)?**
- **It sounds like you're concerned about (high turnover). What can you tell me about that?**
- **Are you worried about…?**
- **What difficulties have you had with…?**
- **How are you handling…?**

Ask questions about the challenges their situation creates.

Use these questions to find out where they hurt… and how you can help.

C. Questions to Clarify Problems

Get more information by responding to their concerns with in-depth questions to expand on their problems.

Use **PowerPhrases to Clarify Problems,** such as:

- **Why is that a problem?**
- **What about that worries you?**
- **What is it about ___ that are you not satisfied with?**
- **Are you having any other difficulties with…?**
- **Tell me more about your problems with…**

Clarification of the problem leads you to the next step, which is to ask questions about the implications of the problems they are describing. Use implication questions to uncover why the problem is important to the buyer.

This gives you more information, and it also makes the buyer more aware of the need.

Use **PowerPhrases to Reveal Implications of Problems,** such as:

- **How do those problems impact other departments?**
- **So does that mean that you…?**
- **Has that affected…?**
- **What is the impact of that problem on…?**
- **Has that led you to…?**
- **What is the result of that?**

Buyers need to become aware of every area that is affected by the problem.

Use questions to find out where they hurt… and how you can help.

Sales professionals uncover and satisfy needs.

PowerPhrases in Unlikely Places

During a recent chat, an old friend mentioned his several million-dollar home and his swimming pool. Since it was hot and I wanted to keep up, I decided to invest in a pool of my own. I wanted one that fit my budget and tolerance for maintenance, so I took my business to KB Toys.

I went in looking for a small blow up pool, and walked out with a large blow up pool, a pool cover, a pump and an array of pool toys.

After asking me about where I live and what I wanted it for, the sales professional (yes, he was a professional!) said:

- **Most people are much happier with the 5'x10' pool. They like the fact that you can actually float on it.**

That, of course, led in for the next up-sell:

- **Meryl, which of the floats will you be getting today?**

After I settled on a float, the skilled sales person asked:

- **Do you already have a pump that will work with that?**

All this time he was taking my selections to the counter. He then pointed out:

- **Meryl, you mentioned that you live in the mountains. That water will get chilly as it cools off at night. You want a cover to keep some of the warmth in, and keep the debris out.**
- **Do you want me to help you pick out the best water toys for your needs?**

I walked out with my arms filled with far more than I had intended to buy, and I was glad that I did. My sales representative was a service professional. He anticipated needs, and made sure I got all those needs met from him, not somewhere else. I offer my compliments to the management of KB Toys in Colorado Springs.

Questions to Focus on the Value of Solving the Problem

You may think that by now both you and they are painfully aware of the problem, and it is time to look for solutions. Take one more step first. Help them to envision life with their problem solved. The next set of PowerPhrases addresses the importance of solving the problem. Help them understand how much better things will be when their problems are solved. Once problems and their implications are determined, use **PowerPhrases to Focus on the Value of Solving the Problem**, such as:

Help them to envision life with their problem solved.

- **How much would you save if you could…?**
- **Imagine if this problem was solved…**
- **How useful would it be for you to be able to…?**
- **If we could ___, how much would that increase your volume?**
- **If I could show you a way to…**
- **How important is it that you…?**
- **How else would it help you to be able to…?**
- **If I could help you to___, what could you do that you can't do now?**
- **What high-priority projects could you free yourself up for if you did not have to spend as much time on…?**
- **What could you do with the savings?**

- **What would it be worth to you to…?**
- **How would (increased output) affect (your profitability)?**

Help the buyer feel the need to solve their problem. Only then will they care at all about the solutions you offer.

Demonstrating Value

You can easily demonstrate value without creating resistance if you do an excellent job of uncovering needs and selling the buyer on the value of solving the problem. Now you are ready to demonstrate the features and the benefits of what you offer.

You can easily demonstrate value without creating resistance if you do an excellent job of uncovering needs and selling the buyer on the value of solving the problem.

Features tell you the facts and characteristics of what you offer. Some features are: the number of pages in a book, the number of minutes included in your phone plan and the amount of memory in a computer. Features are about you and your product.

True benefits address a need that the buyer has clearly stated they want to resolve. Since they have already told you that they want to solve these problems, expressing true benefits prevents objections. Preventing objections eliminates the need to solve objections.

To express benefits, use a **PowerPhrase to Communicate Benefits**, such as:

- **This gives you the ___ you asked for.**
- **Our widgets meet your specifications.**
- **This is comfortably within the budget range you have given us.**
- **We can meet your stated timetable.**
- **You have said that ___ is important, and we meet your need for ___ by___.**

You won't need as many PowerPhrases for describing benefits if you have effectively established the need.

Overcoming Objections

In *Spin Selling,* Neil Rackham asserts that most objections are created when the seller offers solutions too soon. Lay the groundwork first, and brush up on PowerPhrases to handle the objections that you do get.

When they object to price, use a **PowerPhrase to Overcome the Price Objection**, such as:

- **What were you planning to pay?**
- **Why do you say that?**
- **We can lower the price. What would you want to eliminate from the package to do that?**
- **What are you comparing it to?**
- **Does your company always offer the cheapest price? Will you agree that price is not always the only consideration?**
- **My grandmother used to say that quality is remembered long after cost is forgotten.**
- **What is the cost of (their problem)?**
- **Is money the only problem here?**
- **I hear that from time to time from people before they invest. I never hear that from those who have made the investment.**
- **Let's bring it down to the cost per day.**
- **Have you ever paid more than you planned for something you wanted and been glad that you did?**

If their objection is that they want to stay with their current supplier, use a **PowerPhrase to Convince Them to Change Suppliers**, such as:

- **If I can show you that ours is better, you would want to consider changing or at least sampling what we offer, wouldn't you?**
- **Isn't it worth the trouble to change if we offer more?**

Objections are created when the seller offers solutions too soon. Lay the groundwork first.

- I appreciate your loyalty. I believe you deserve to have a better (service, product).
- Isn't your first loyalty to the company?
- Times have changed, and what worked before may not be what is best now.
- Why not give us a small order to check us out?
- Many of our best customers were reluctant to make the change at first. May I tell you why they are glad that they switched?
- Is there anything about your current supplier that you are not totally happy with? If we could eliminate the problem, wouldn't it be worth considering?
- That's why I need to work extra hard to earn and keep your business.
- Why not give us a chance?
- Change is not comfortable, but it is necessary to stay ahead of the competition.
- Wouldn't it make sense to have an alternative source?
- I am not asking for all of your business here.

Often potential buyers will tell you that they need to think it over because they have not yet heard what they need to be ready to buy.

Another common objection is the "think it over" objection.

Use a **PowerPhrase to Overcome the Think It Over Objection**, such as:

- Can you think it over out loud so I can help?
- What do we need to think about?
- What concerns do you have?
- Let's think about it together.
- What do you need from me that would enable you to make a decision now?
- It is possible to think too long. Procrastination can cost money.

- **What is your reason for saying that?**
- **Is there anything I haven't explained well enough?**
- **You want to think about it? Many people do, and what they consistently find is that their greatest regret is that they did not act sooner.**

While the need to reflect on a deal can be legitimate, often potential buyers will tell you that they need to think it over because they have not yet heard what they need to be ready to buy. The above PowerPhrases will help you uncover the real issues.

Closing Phrases

Closing phrases begin with trial closes. These are questions that examine the readiness of the buyer to take action. If you get a yes, you have a sale. If you get a no, you gain information that tells you where you need to focus to reach the sale. Test their readiness in a way that does not force them to take a concrete stand. If you go for a firm commitment too soon, they might get backed into a corner that they cannot come out of without losing face.

Trial closes examine the readiness of the buyer to take action.

Some **Trial PowerPhrase Closes to Test the Readiness of the Buyer,** are:

- **What do you think of what I've told you so far?**
- **Which version best suits your needs?**
- **On a scale of 1 to 10, with 10 being ready to invest, where are you? What would it take to get you to a 10?**
- **Do you prefer this one or that one?**
- **Wouldn't you agree that this is what you want?**
- **Doesn't this meet all of the specifications you provided?**
- **I believe that this meets your needs. Do you agree?**
- **Why not give it a try?**

- **Doesn't it make you feel secure to have something that will allow you to…?**
- **Does this meet all the needs you described?**
- **What can I do to get your business?**
- **If you were me, what would you do now?**
- **Do you need to consult anyone before placing an order?**
- **This is what you want, isn't it?**
- **Are there any questions I haven't answered?**
- **What do you think?**

If you get a positive response to these questions, you have a sale. Go for the actual close. At this point, do not hint or beat around the bush.

Clearly ask, using a **PowerPhrase to Close the Sale,** such as:

Before you leave a sales call, use a PowerPhrase to ask for referrals.

- **How do you spell your name?**
- **How do you want to take care of the cost?**
- **Will that be cash or charge?**
- **Let's get started.**
- **Let's make the decision now.**
- **If you want it, you've got it.**
- **I just need you to okay this right here.**
- **I'll keep the paperwork as simple as possible.**
- **Let's get the paperwork started now.**
- **Let's wrap it up so we can lock in your rate.**

Congratulations! You PowerPhrased your way into a successful sale! You're done now, right?

Well, not quite. You still need to ask for referrals.

PowerPhrases to Request Referrals

Of course, what you REALLY want to do now is to get

out of there fast before they change their minds, grab a cool one, sit back and tell your friends about the big one you caught.

Don't do that just yet. Before you leave, use a **PowerPhrase to Ask for Referrals,** such as:

- **Who do you know who also could benefit from this service?**
- **I would appreciate the names of some of your acquaintances who could find value in what I offer.**
- **Before I leave, I need one more thing from you. Will you please tell me whom else you know…?**
- **If you were me, whom else would you call?**

NOW you can get out of there and celebrate! You earned it!

Celebrate! You earned it!

EXERCISES

I have a warning for you before you begin this exercise. It might seem laborious and tedious. I thought that when I first did it, but it helped me to realize where I was unprepared for the selling that I do. After I set out the exercises for you, I apply the exercises with an example from my own career. If you get lost, use that as a reference.

Step 1. Think about a product or service you offer. List five features of this product.

1. ______________________________
2. ______________________________
3. ______________________________
4. ______________________________
5. ______________________________

Step 2. Next, list five benefits in terms of problems the features can solve for a buyer.

1. ______________________________
2. ______________________________
3. ______________________________
4. ______________________________
5. ______________________________

Step 3. What need would make a buyer care about those benefits?

1. ______________________________
   ____
2. ______________________________
   ____
3. ______________________________
   ____
4. ______________________________
   ____

5. ____

____

Step 4. What situations would lead to those needs?

1. ____

____

2. ____

____

3. ____

____

4. ____

____

5. ____

____

Step 5. What PowerPhrases could you use to determine their situations and needs?

1. ____

____

2. ____

____

3. ____

____

4. ____

____

5. ____

____

Step 6. What PowerPhrases could you use to uncover the problems?

1. ____

____

2. ____

____

3. ____

____

4. ____

____

5. ____

____

Step 7. What PowerPhrases could you use to clarify those problems?

1. ____

____

2. ____

____

3. ____

____

4. ____

____

5. ____

____

Step 8. They need to feel the full implications of their problem before they are motivated to solve it. What PowerPhrases would you use to uncover those implications?

1. ____

____

2. ____

____

3. ____

____

4. ____

____

5. ____

____

Step 9. The next step is to get them to focus on the importance and value of solving the problem. What PowerPhrases do you use for that?

1. ____

____

2. ____

____

3. ____

____

4. ____

____

5. ____

____

Step 10. Now they are ready to hear the benefits. How can you express the benefits in a way that ties into their specific needs?

1. ____

____

2. ____

____

3. ____

____

4. ____

____

5. ____

____

Sample Exercise

At seminars, I sell a powerful tape set called *12 Secrets to High Self-Esteem* by Linda Larsen.[5] I honestly believe that if people do not walk out of the room with those tapes, it is because I did not use my PowerPhrases well enough. Here is how I apply the process.

Step 1. Features:

1. Six cassettes.
2. Workbook.
3. 12 specific steps.
4. Uses stories, research and examples.
5. Describes goal setting.

Step 2. Benefits, problems it can solve:

1. Fear of asking for what you want.
2. Putting yourself down.
3. Overreacting emotionally.
4. Confusion about what you want in life.
5. Settling for less than you deserve.

Step 3. In order to care, a buyer would have to feel a need for:

1. Assertive communications skills.
2. Self-acceptance.
3. Emotional control.
4. Goal clarification.
5. A sense of deserving.

Step 4. Situations that would lead to these needs are:

1. No good training or role models. Being told "Don't you talk back to me!"
2. Critical people.
3. Emotionally repressive or reactive environments. Environments where telling the truth about your feelings is unsafe.
4. Others expecting their needs to be consistently first.
5. Experiencing conditional love. Abusive relationships.

[5] *12 Secrets of High Self Esteem*, Larsen, Linda, SkillPath Publications

Step 5. PowerPhrases to Determine Situation:

- How did you learn to ask for what you want?
- Were any of your immediate family critical of you?
- Are you able to express emotions calmly in an honest and open way?
- Have you ever been expected to sacrifice what you want for someone else and later resented it?
- Have you ever felt taken advantage of?

Step 6. PowerPhrases to Uncover the Problem:

- Does lack of assertive communication skills ever cause a problem for you?
- Do you tell yourself the same things those critical people tell or told you?
- What challenges has lack of emotional control created for you?
- How satisfied are you with your history of setting personal goals and reaching them?
- What has being taken advantage of cost you?

Step 7. PowerPhrases to Clarify Problems:

- What other problems have you had due to lack of assertiveness?
- What has been the result of those negative conversations in your head?
- Is emotional control a problem for you in other areas of your life as well?
- What about your lack of goal setting worries you?
- Have you had other difficulties with being taken advantage of?

Step 8. PowerPhrases to Reveal Implications of Problems:

- Has your lack of assertiveness created problems for your family as well?
- Do the negative conversations in your head keep you from going after what you want?
- Does that emotional control problem ever cause your staff to be afraid to discuss issues with you?
- Does your lack of direction frustrate your family?
- Does being vulnerable to being taken advantage of ever cause you to keep people at arms length?

Step 9. PowerPhrase to Focus on the Value of Solving the Problem:

- How important is it that you learn to assert yourself?
- What difference would it make in your life if you were not second-guessing yourself?
- If you had better emotional control, how would your life be better?
- If you began setting goals toward the things you dream about, where do you picture yourself in five years?
- How would your life improve if you learned to set clear boundaries?

Step 10. PowerPhrases to Sell the Benefits of Your Product:

- Secret number nine in the *12 Secrets to High Self-Esteem* is "Communicating with Confidence." It gives you the exact assertiveness skills you said you need to…
- You can get (what they said they would get if they stopped second-guessing themselves) by investing in the *12 Secrets to High Self-Esteem.* "Accessing Your Internal Wisdom" is secret number two. That and secret number four, "Accepting Yourself and Letting Go of the Past" will give you the self acceptance you said would free you to do what you want.
- Linda Larsen will tell you exactly what to do to get the emotional control you said would help you (the benefits they mentioned) with secret 5, "Managing Your Emotions."
- You said you see yourself being ___ in five years if you improve your goal setting. Linda Larsen will tell you exactly how to get there.
- The *12 Secrets* will show you how to get that life you envision when you learn to set clear boundaries.

Using these steps is tedious at first, but over time the framework becomes automatic.

QUIZ

1. Which type of PowerPhrase needs to be used sparingly and only in the beginning?

____

2. Which type of PowerPhrase do you need to avoid using too soon in the selling process?

____

Answers:

1. Situation questions need to be used sparingly and only in the beginning. Too many of these imply that you haven't done your homework.

2. PowerPhrases to communicate benefits need to be reserved until the need is clearly established. Let the buyer "feel their pain" first.

Chapter 7

Small Talk PowerPhrases™ to Break the Ice

Do you look forward to social situations where you are expected to strike up conversations with people you do not know? Or would you rather have a tax audit, drink cod liver oil, or get a root canal?

If you dread small talk, you are not alone. You may have heard that the greatest fear of most people is speaking in public. Did you know that our second greatest fear is starting a conversation with someone we do not know? If you are not comfortable with it, it might help to know that six out of those eight people you meet are not comfortable with it either.

The second greatest fear of all is starting a conversation with someone we do not know.

The really good news is that the art of mingling is a learned one. Like any other skill, you can master it. You can learn the lines that melt the ice. I'm talking PowerPhrases here, if you haven't guessed!

Do you think small talk is a waste of time? The truth is that small talk is anything BUT a waste of time. If you have two people with equal skills, who is likely to get the promotion–the one who is shy and retreated, keeping to herself but doing a great job–or the other who jokes easily with the CEO as well as the janitor, knows who to call to get things done in a hurry, and who is on a first name basis with the entire Chamber of Commerce and Rotary club and is also doing a great job? Small talk makes big things happen! Small talk turns strangers into acquaintances, and acquaintances into friends. People like doing business with their friends.

How to Begin

The most important PowerPhrase available is the other person's name. Use it freely–and with care. If you meet Susan, David, Barbara and Robert, don't say:

— *Hey Susie!*

— *Nice to meet you Dave!*

— *Barb, how are you?*

— *Bob, it's a pleasure!*

Call them Susan, David, Barbara and Robert until you have been given permission to alter it. If there is any doubt about whether to use first names or surnames, use their surnames–or ask!

Small talk makes big things happen!

Take the time to learn the correct pronunciation. Help them with yours!

Use a **PowerPhrase to Help Others to Pronounce and Remember Your Name,** such as:

- **Hi! I'm Meryl Runion. Meryl rhymes with barrel and Runion rhymes with onion. So if you forget my name, think about a barrel of onions.**
- **I'm Houston Rose. Houston is like the city, Rose is like the flower.**

If you meet someone who has a difficult name, do not pretend that they do not have a name! Take the time to get their name right. If you are unsure of the pronunciation, ask for their help in remembering it.

Simply use a **PowerPhrase to Get Help Remembering a Name,** such as:

- **What a lovely name. I want to be certain that I say it correctly. What tips do you have for me?**

Take the responsibility of names onto yourself. If you

have forgotten someone's name, use a **PowerPhrase to Ask That a Name Be Repeated,** such as:

- **I'm sorry; I've forgotten your name.**
- **What was your name again?**
- **You don't happen to remember YOUR name, do you?**
- **Please help me out. I've gone blank here.**

If you think they may have forgotten your name, tell them before they have to ask. Say:

- **Janet, Meryl Runion, how are you?**

You can also prompt them to tell you their name by greeting them with a reminder of your name.

Learning Names Through Repetition

Repeat their names as much as possible. Don't say:

— *What was that like?*

when you can say:

- **Janet, what was that like?**

Every time you use their name, it adds to the rapport between you, and it reinforces their name in your mind.

Every time you use their name, it adds to the rapport between you.

Giving More Information in Order to Invite More Information From Them

Be aware that people usually respond in kind to the way we speak to them. If I say:

— *Hi! I'm Meryl!*

they are likely to say:

— *Hi! I'm ___.*

If I say:

- **Hi! I'm Meryl Runion and I'm a speaker and an author. I'm here for the first time.**

they are likely to say:

- **I'm ___ ___, and I work for Widget Wonderland. I've been coming since August.**

Now I have some information to work with! I know they work for Widget Wonderland and they have been coming since last August. I can use that to ask questions that will open the conversation up further.

- **Widget Wonderland! I haven't been there since it was Widget Wonder World. How has it changed?**
- **What have you gained from coming here?**

Keep going until you forget that small talk is something you're not good at.

The art of mingling is a learned one.

Power Pointer–Small Talk PowerPhrases on an Airplane

On a flight I took recently, a flight attendant showed a remarkable ability to start conversations. She asked me if my top was silk, and went on to tell me about how her boyfriend put her silk clothes through the washer and dryer. Of course, I had ruined-clothes-stories of my own. She was chatting casually with everyone in the same way.

Most of us make similar associations in response to other people, but only a few of us actually think to relay our associations to strangers. This flight attendant's gift was the casualness with which she relayed her inner experience. Her absolute comfort with it made it comfortable for everyone else as well.

Small talk is much easier if you are interested in what the other person has to say. There is something interesting in everyone. Relax and consider yourself an undercover agent with a mission to find out what is interesting about them.

Starting Conversations With Statements

Do you ever attempt to start a conversation with a statement?

— *Great weather we're having.*

— *The turnout is huge here today!*

If you think you are throwing out a conversational ball that they should pick up and toss back, think again. Statements like these lead nowhere unless you are talking to a small talk genius that knows how to pick the ball up and toss it back. Remember that most people respond at the same level we put things out? Most people will not pick up that ball and toss it back. Give them something they can get their hands on.

The Three-Step Ice-Breaking Process

Use the three-step ice breaking process.

Instead of throwing out a statement and hoping that they will pick up on it, use the three-step ice breaking process.

1. Make an opening statement.
2. Reveal something (not too personal) about your self. (Usually they will respond by giving you information about themselves.)
3. Encourage them to reveal something about them selves.

Good opening statements come from observing the environment or the other person. Good disclosure statements come from observing yourself and your thoughts. Good invitation questions come from a genuine interest in the other person and/or the information they can give you.

Put them together into the three-step ice-breaking process.

Statement	Disclosure	Invitation
That's a beautiful painting!	I don't know much about art.	What kind of art do you like?
This food is delicious.	I like Indian food.	How about you?
Great house!	I like southwestern styling.	How did you come up with the theme?
The elevator is taking forever.	I'm going to be late to my seminar.	What are you here for?
Great weather we're having.	This weather makes me wish I still had my motorcycle.	How do you take advantage of weather like this?
The turnout is huge here today!	I came to hear the talk on eWidgets.	What brings you here?

Open-ended Questions

Closed-ended questions give the other person nowhere to go.

Have you ever attempted to initiate small talk with closed-ended questions that give the other person nowhere to go? Don't ask:

— *What do you do?*

— *How was your vacation?*

— *How are you?*

— *Where do you live?*

These questions solicit one-word responses. They are useful if you are looking for specific information, but they do not draw the other person out. They are only useful as small talk if you follow them up with open-ended questions. Otherwise, after they've said I'm an attorney, fine, downtown and great, what are you left with?

Open-ended questions are more effective. These are the questions that require a more extensive response. Open-ended questions are **PowerPhrases That Get a Conversation Going,** such as:

- **What led you to do the kind of work you are doing?**
- **What did you like best about your vacation?**
- **What do you like about where you live?**
- **Get me up-to-date on what's been happening for you lately.**
- **How did you get started in your business?**
- **What do you enjoy most about the work you do?**
- **What advice would you give someone just starting in your business?**
- **How has your industry changed lately?**
- **What separates you from your competition?**

Before you speak, ask yourself how you would respond to the remark if someone made it to you. If the answer is that your response would not provide much new information, find another way to express yourself.

Open-ended questions require more extensive responses.

Closed-ended questions often begin with:

— *How long…*

— *Have you…*

— *Do you…*

— *Would you…*

— *Did you…*

Open-ended questions often begin with **PowerPhrase Sentence Stems to Open a Conversation**, such as:

- **What about…**
- **Explain…**
- **Tell me about…**
- **What do you…?**
- **What got you…?**
- **Describe…**

Beware of questions that begin with why. "Why" questions can trigger a defensive response in your listener.

Develop a 10-Second Commercial for Yourself

Prepare yourself for meeting strangers by planning a 10-second commercial for yourself. When you introduce yourself, give additional information. That gives them information to work with in developing and keeping a conversation going. Chances are excellent that they will then offer more information back.

If David says he is a systems engineer, his listener might not know what to say next. Listeners might have an easier time if he uses a **10-Second Commercial PowerPhrase,** such as:

- **I'm a systems engineer. When someone wants to do something the computer refuses to do, they call me. My job is to analyze how to get the computer to do it.**

Plan a 10-second commercial for yourself.

When I explain that I am a speaker and an author, people often do not have much of a picture of what I do. They have more to work with if I use my **10-Second Commercial PowerPhrase.**

- **I teach conflict resolution and other success skills to companies and in public seminars. Also, I'm writing a book called** ***PowerPhrases!*****.**

You know from experience what common questions people ask you, so answer those questions for them up front. Prepare in advance.

You may have met network-marketing people who respond to the question, "What do you do?" by saying:

— *I help people start businesses.*

This is misleading and unclear. You want to add clarity, not confusion.

A good **10-Second Commercial PowerPhrase** for this

situation might be:

- **I have a wellness business. I market magnets for health and pain control, and I help others with their wellness businesses as well.**

The main key is to prepare. When you go to an event where there is likely to be small talk, plan your PowerPhrases in advance. Read the paper, survey the environment, and come up with interesting topics for discussion.

Know What You Have to Give and What You Want to Get

Go into networking situations and make small talk with a clear idea of what you want to accomplish–and what you have to give. Every person you meet needs to know something that you already know, and every person you meet knows something that you need to know. If you begin your small talk with a clear idea of how you want the conversation to end up, you are likely to have satisfying results. Be straightforward about what you are looking for by using a **PowerPhrase to Make Your Agenda Known,** such as:

Begin your small talk with a clear idea of how you want the conversation to end up.

- **I would like to get to know you better because…**
- **I am here because I am looking for information about…**
- **I am looking for information about… Do you know someone who can help me?**

You are creating a give and get situation. If no one makes his or her needs known, no one will give and no one will get.

There is nothing small and insignificant about small talk. Take the time to learn the art. And before you attend a networking situation, be certain to prepare.

Exercises

1. Turn the following closed-ended questions into open-ended questions.

Are things changing a lot in your department?

____

____

Is your job challenging?

____

____

Do you come here often?

____

____

2. Create a 10-Second Commercial for Yourself

____

____

____

____

____

____

____

____

____

____

____

____

____

____

____

Chapter 8

PowerPhrases™ at Work: Managing Your Boss

Have you seen the lists of buzzwords that you can choose from if you want to sound "erudite"? There are three columns of words. You are instructed to pick a word from each column, and you end up with statements like:

— *ineluctable semidiurnal factionalism, or:*

— *facilitating cognizant circumlocution.*

The results are big expressions with very little meaning. The trend in governments and businesses is toward simpler and more straightforward communications. There are plenty of exceptions however. Until recently the Minneapolis airport played a message that said:

— *Attention passengers! Please carefully control your bags to avoid the unauthorized introduction of foreign objects by unknown persons.*

I always picture a harried passenger shouting "Down bags!" to their out-of-control bags. There is an "unknown person," dressed in black and wearing a ski mask, introducing foreign objects–Chinese coins and Russian nesting dolls–into the out-of-control bags. How about a simple "Watch your bags so that strangers don't put anything in them"?

That sounds like a PowerPhrase to me!

The trend in governments and businesses is toward simpler and more straightforward communications.

Your business communications need to be clear and direct at work, starting at the interview.

PowerPhrases at the Interview

Does it seem odd to you that PowerPhrases have a place in a job interview? Job interviews are about selling yourself. How can you sell yourself with memorized phrases that you read in a book? The answer is that you don't simply memorize anything. You adapt the PowerPhrases to your own situation. The PowerPhrases get you started-and you take it from there. You will do much better if you are prepared for common interview questions.

Prepare responses in advance for common interview questions.

Power Preparation for the Interview

In addition to preparing your PowerPhrases, learn everything you can about the company. Read their web pages, annual report, journals and newsletters. Talk to everyone that you know who knows anything about the company. Also be certain to request a job description for the position you are applying for so you can prepare to show them how you can meet their needs.

PowerPhrase Responses to Common Interview Questions

A very popular ice-breaking interview question is: "Tell me about yourself."

Don't say:

— *My name is… and I come from…*

— *My hobbies are…*

— *What I like to do best is…*

Instead, be specific and use a **PowerPhrase for**

Describing Yourself, such as:

- **My strengths are… An example is…**
- **My accomplishments are… For example…**
- **My greatest area of knowledge is… I have used this by…**

Or ask:

- **Is there a particular area you would like for me to discuss?**

Use strong words, and then illustrate them with specifics.

When asked why you are in the job market, don't say:

— *They didn't appreciate me where I was.*

— *My boss was an idiot.*

— *I did not like it.*

— *I was personally responsible for the company declaring bankruptcy.*

Use strong words, and then illustrate them with specifics.

Instead use a **PowerPhrase for Explaining Why You Are in the Job Market**, such as:

- **I have a plan for my career. I need a place that offers opportunity for growth.**
- **I am ready for a new set of challenges.**
- **I want a job that I can give my all to and that I can stay in for a long time. I'm looking for the right opportunity.**

When they ask why you are the best person for the job, don't say:

— *I think this is a good place to work.*

— *Nothing else looked interesting.*

— *I'm out of work.*

— *I don't know for sure that I am because I haven't met the other candidates.*

Instead, use a **PowerPhrase for Explaining Why You Are the Best for the Job,** such as:

- **I put my heart into everything I do. For example...**
- **I thrive on problem solving and challenges. For example...**
- **You need someone who can produce results. My track record shows that I am that kind of a person.**
- **This job is exactly what I want. What I can do for you is...**
- **My experience demonstrates my versatility.**

Even if you are uncertain about being the best candidate, speak with confidence.

Even if you are uncertain, speak with confidence.

Power Thinking to the Rescue–Replace Limiting Thinking With Power Thoughts

You want to have an attitude of confidence at the interview, and the attitude you project will be a reflection of your thoughts.

Don't think:

— Why would they choose me?

— I need to prove myself to them.

— They aren't going to like me.

These thoughts will make you appear weak and needy. Instead, think:

- **I have much to offer.**
- **This is an opportunity to find out if we are a match.**
- **I am here to learn about them as well as for them to learn about me.**

The second set of thoughts will make you appear confident and calm.

Asking the Interviewer PowerPhrase Questions

Do you dread job interviews? Think of them as two-way streets rather than one-way interrogations. Job interviews are not just about the potential employer finding out if you meet their needs. Both the employer and the job seeker want a good match. You're not just along for the ride at an interview. Be prepared to shine. Also, be prepared to seek the information you need to make a knowledgeable career decision. When the interviewer asks if you have questions, don't say:

— *No. (Implies that you don't really care.)*

Avoid asking questions that imply that you are only interested in what you can get. Also avoid questions that have a negative spin and questions that indicate that you haven't done your homework, such as:

— *How much will you pay me? (Only interested in what you can get)*

— *What happened to the person who had the job before me? (Negative)*

— *What does this company do, anyway? (Under-prepared)*

Be prepared to seek the information you need to make a knowledgeable career decision.

You need to be prepared with **PowerPhrase Questions for the Interviewer**, such as:

- **What else can I tell you about my qualifications?**
- **What are the initial responsibilities of the position?**
- **What problems face your staff?**
- **What is the growth potential in this position?**
- **How long have you been here? What do you like about the company?**
- **What would the characteristics and experience of the perfect applicant be?**
- **What is the mission of the company?**

Show your interest and initiative in the questions that you ask. If you do not ask questions, you imply that you take whatever someone hands you. Your first job is to be responsive to the interviewer. Your second job is to guide the interview as needed.

When the interview is winding down, use PowerPhrases to get closure.

Going for Closure With PowerPhrases Without Being Pushy.

Do not leave the interview without going for some closure. Toward the end of the interview, create a sense of value and urgency by using **PowerPhrases That Push for Action.**

Show your interest and initiative in the questions that you ask. If you do not ask questions, you imply that you take whatever someone hands you.

- **Are there any qualities you are looking for that you haven't seen in me?**
- **Is there anything you want to know that I haven't told you?**
- **What can I tell you that would prompt you to make an offer now?**
- **Can you offer me the job?**

If they say no, ask:

- **Can you refer me to someone who can use my skills?**

If they say they will consider the application and get back to you, say:

- **When can I expect your decision?**
- **If I have not heard from you by then, may I call you?**

A PowerPhrase to the Rescue! Take Charge Without Taking Control!

I was interviewing for a job that I was seriously under-qualified for. The interviewer was talking about everything but the job! I felt discouraged and out-of-control. I did not get the job. I was told what I could do to improve my qualifications and that if I cared to reapply in about a year, they would reconsider my application.

One year later and slightly more qualified, I interviewed again with the same interviewer. It was like history revisited. The interviewer was off on a tangent. This time, rather than panic, I took charge. This time I said:

- **I want to focus on the job, because this is what I want to do.**

I could see it in the interviewer's eyes. That was the moment I got the job.

Many employers are looking for assertive candidates. That can be demonstrated by how assertive you are willing to be with them.

Most employers are looking for assertive candidates. This can be demonstrated by how assertive you are willing to be with them.

PowerPhrases for When You Are New on the Job

Once you have the job, use PowerPhrases to help you to integrate into your new environment. While you want to look good those early weeks, you don't want to alienate anyone or come across as arrogant.

Don't say:

— *That's not how we did it at Widget Direct.*

Use **PowerPhrases for Your Early Days on the Job,**

such as:

- **I'm looking forward to understanding how you do it here.**
- **I am happy to try it your way.**

Don't say:

— *Let me tell you all about myself!*

Say:

- **I'm anxious to learn about you.**

Don't say:

— *I can figure it out myself.*

Say:

- **I need your help.**
- **I need your advice.**
- **I can use some input here.**

PowerPhrases help you to integrate into your new environment.

When you make inevitable errors or don't know what is expected of you, don't say:

— *I'm only human!*

— *Be nice to me, I'm new.*

— *I haven't got the experience.*

Use **PowerPhrases for Reminding Them That You Are New**, such as:

- **I'm sorry. I am still in my learning curve.**
- **I just made another mistake to learn from.**
- **That is the last time I will make that mistake!**

Do not wait for them to tell you everything. **Use PowerPhrase Questions for New Employees,** such as:

- **How can I help?**
- **What more can I do?**
- **How am I doing?**
- **What are my priorities?**

Also, refer to them as:

- **Mr. or Ms.**

until told otherwise.

PowerPhrases for Your Supervisor

In the Beginning

Your first meeting with your boss sets the tone for your entire working relationship, so plan ahead for that. Much of the initial weeks are about getting to know your boss. Time spent getting to know your boss is time well invested. Since you are likely to get a new boss every six months, it is important to know the PowerPhrases involved. Do not expect to be at full capacity your first day. Do not say:

— *This isn't what I was hired to do.*

— *When are you going to tell me what to do?*

— *I don't have a plan, that's your job.*

Time spent getting to know your boss is time well invested.

Use **PowerPhrases for Meeting Your Boss**, such as:

- **I'm _____ and am looking forward to working with you.**
- **Can you give me a quick sense of the priorities in the department?**
- **When you have a chance, I have some action ideas of my own that I would like your opinion on.**

Every manager has their own idea of how things should be done. You need to study your manager's style. Ask questions about how your boss wants things.

Don't say:

— *This isn't how my old boss did things.*

— *You need to tell me what to do.*

— *I have my own way of doing things.*

Instead, ask questions and make remarks such as the following **PowerPhrases for Getting to Know Your Boss.**

- **What more can I do to help you?**
- **I look forward to understanding your style.**
- **I want to learn what you need from me.**
- **May I take notes?**
- **What did you particularly like about the way the last person who had this position did the job?**
- **I'd like to know more about you in order to best understand how to work with you.**

First you learn them – then they learn you.

Power Pointer–First You Learn Them –Then They Learn You.

One group of assistants agreed: when you begin a job, you need to learn your boss' style. Then help the boss learn yours. Once you know your boss' preferences, strengths and limitations, develop systems to work with them. Once they are developed, you can introduce them to your supervisor bit by bit.

Making Suggestions to Your Boss

Some bosses are very open to new ideas. Others like to think that everything is their idea. There are ways to make recommendations that leave them thinking that they thought of it.

If they like to think that they thought of everything, don't say:

— *My advice is…*

— *Obviously you should…*

— *Try this…*

Instead, use a **PowerPhrase for Making Suggestions to the Boss,** such as:

- **Have you considered...?**
- **Something you said the other day got me thinking...**
- **I'd like your opinion about what I did with the concepts you and I discussed last month.**

Power Pointer–Always Look for Something to Agree About.

Bob had a product line designed exclusively for his department. When Bob's director encouraged selling the line through the call center, Bob said:

- **Short term that makes a lot of sense. Here are the problems I see long term.**

Note Bob refrained from saying:

– *That's short-term smart and long term dumb.*

His opening acknowledged the validity of the perspective but led into the second part, which outlined what the boss had not considered.

Some bosses like to think that everything is their idea.

Do you hesitate to offer suggestions when you completely disagree with the boss? According to my informal polls, about one out of three adults equate disagreement with conflict. The better worded a disagreement is, the easier it is to bypass the sense of being in conflict.

Don't say:

— *You're wrong.*

— *You shouldn't see it that way.*

— *I disagree.*

Instead use a **PowerPhrase for Disagreeing With the**

Boss, such as:

- **Help me to understand how you reached that conclusion.**
- **I wonder if we have the same information. My information leads me to a different conclusion.**
- **I want to give my best here. I can support you better if we can resolve these differences first.**

Replace Limiting Thinking With Power Thoughts

If you view your disagreement as a conflict, conflict is more likely to result. Don't think:

— *It's me against him/her.*

— *I'm not a team player if I refuse.*

Think:

- **We can work toward an effective solution here.**
- **My assessment of what is possible is important information for the boss.**
- **My needs are important too.**

Have a fallback position if the boss does not appreciate your candor.

- **I know that you are the boss and I will do whatever you say.**

It is not your manager's job to keep track of what assignments you have been given.

Refusing Assignments

Do you have the right to refuse an assignment? Absolutely! It is not your manager's job to keep track of what assignments you have been given. Often they don't know what else you have to do. When you refuse an assignment, don't say:

— *I can't.*

– *I don't have the skills.*
– *I'm overloaded already.*
– *Why do I get all the crummy assignments?*
– *What do I look like here, wonder woman/superman?*

Begin by clarifying the request. Ask detailed questions so you know the scope.

Be certain to ask the following **PowerPhrases for Clarifying an Assignment**, such as:

- **I need some more information. What is the deadline?**
- **I need some more information. What budget is allotted?**
- **I need some more information. What are the specifications?**
- **Which is the most binding of the three, and how flexible are the others?**

Use a PowerPhrase for refusing an assignment.

If you decide from the answers that you cannot carry out the assignment, use a **PowerPhrase for Refusing an Assignment.** This phrase will follow the same format for saying no as was described in Chapter 3. Begin with an acknowledgment, explain the situation, and reaffirm the relationship by presenting options.

Refusing Assignments With the Three-Step Process for Saying "No"

Acknowledge	Circumstance	Transform
This project is so important it needs someone who can make it his or her top priority.	I have the following projects and dead-lines…	Let me look into it and come back with a list of questions and recommendations.
I am flattered that you considered me for this assignment.	After reviewing it I see some problems that need to be reviewed before proceeding.	Let's discuss the prob-lems I see and what options we can create.
I take this project very seriously.	The risk I see in my taking this on is…	If we can resolve these I will be happy to take this on.
I would prefer to say yes to every assign-ment you offer me.	My concerns are…	What can I put aside to free myself up for this?

Use the three-step process for saying "No" when you need to refuse an assignment.

You can also use a one or two-part format to refuse the assignment.

Saying No in One or Two Parts

Acknowledge	Circumstance	Transform
		Let me look into it and come back with a list of questions and recommendations.
This project is so important it needs someone who can make it his or her top priority.		Have you considered asking…?
	I have reviewed the assignment and see that we have some problems that need to be resolved before proceeding.	What can I put aside to clear my schedule enough to take this on?
		What can I put aside to free myself up for this?
	My policy is not to take on a project without making the risks known. Some of the risks I see to you here are...	

When considering an assignment, ask for more information.

Handling Multiple Supervisors

Do you work for more than one supervisor? Is it a nightmare of competing requests? If so, develop a system that your supervisors agree to in advance. Refer to that system to keep you out of the middle.

Don't say:

— *Take a number.*

— *I can't help you.*

— *Your project is not my only priority.*

— *You're not the only one I support here.*

Instead, use a **PowerPhrase for Managing Work From Multiple Bosses**, such as:

Acknowledge	Circumstance	Transform
I would love to help.	Mary has already scheduled my time.	Why not talk to Mary? Perhaps she can give you priority.
	According to the system we established, I prioritize work by...	I will be able to get to this by....

Develop a system of work prioritization that your supervisors agree to in advance.

Replace Limiting Thinking With Power Thoughts

When managers conflict on priorities, stay out of the middle.

Don't think:

— *I've got to balance all their conflicting demands.*

— *It's up to me to figure this out.*

Think:

- **Their conflicts are between them and I will allow them to resolve them.**
- **We can develop systems that everyone agrees to and I will follow them.**

Meeting With Your Managers

Is getting a meeting with your boss harder than getting a recount in Florida? Meeting with staff is a high-payoff activity for bosses, but supervisors often need to be convinced. Ask for the meetings you need with your boss, but do it with grace. Don't say:

— *You never have enough time for me.*

— *Everything else comes first.*

— *It seems like I don't matter.*

Instead, use a **PowerPhrase for Requesting Regular Meetings With Your Boss,** such as:

- **If we meet for ten minutes on a daily basis, I won't need to interrupt you as frequently throughout the day.**
- **I have found in the past that meeting on a daily basis increases my productivity and allows me to stay in tune with you. It helps me make you look good.**
- **Let's try meeting on a daily basis, monitor the results and see if it is something we would like to continue.**

Also, advocate for regular performance reviews. You need regular reviews to make your supervisors aware of the ways you contribute to the company. In addition, it is in your interest to find out where you fall short of the supervisor's expectations early enough to use the information for change. Don't say:

Ask for the meetings you need with your boss, but do it with grace.

— *I'm afraid I may be doing something wrong.*

— *You promised!*

— *I'm low on the totem poll here.*

Instead use a **PowerPhrase for Requesting a Performance Review,** such as:

- **To give my best possible I would like to set a time to review my progress and set some goals. When can we do that?**
- **I work best with regular feedback, and I want to do the best job possible here.**

Replace Limiting Thinking With Power Thoughts

Performance reviews are opportunities to advance. Don't think:

— I'm afraid of what they might say.

Think:

- **This is a chance to get credit for what I've done and learn what I need to improve.**

The International Association of Administrative Professionals recommends that you gather your information for your supervisor, and have a cover letter saying something like:

You need regular performance reviews to make your supervisors aware of your contributions to the company.

- **Thank you for your role in helping me perform so well in this past year. Some things I appreciate about our working relationship are…**[6]

Be an active participant at your performance review! Performance reviews are wonderful ways to get what you need. Use them to get your accomplishments noticed. Accept praise, consider the criticism and be prepared with facts that make note of your accomplishments.

Use **PowerPhrases for Making Your Accomplishments Known in a Performance Review**, such as:

- **May I begin by telling you the accomplishments I am most proud of?**
- **Here is how I made money for the company…**
- **Here is how I saved money for the company…**
- **Here are three problems I faced last year. What I did to resolve them is…**
- **I want to invite you to tell me what you are most pleased about.**

Be sure to use the review as an opportunity to find out

[6] International Association of Administration Professionals (IAAP) website

what the boss sees as good performance, and what it takes to get a promotion.

- **My understanding is that my priority is to (reconfigure widgets). I have been (assembling 257 per day). Is this the best use of my time?**
- **I want to know in detail what the measurements of good performance are.**
- **What can I do differently to meet your requirements?**

Even weaknesses can be turned in to strengths at performance reviews.

- **Here are some of the areas I have been weak. Here is what I am doing to overcome them.**
- **I realized I was weak in accounting so I took classes.**

Summarize your understanding.

- **My understanding is that I am in good shape and you want me to...(start assembling wind-up widgets). Is this correct?**

Be an active participant at your performance review!

Accepting Feedback

You can expect that during your performance review, you will receive some praise and you can expect that you will receive some criticism. How do you accept praise and criticism from your employer? When praised, don't say:

— *It was nothing.*

— *It was my team. (Unless it was!)*

— *You're right; I did do a great job! Let me tell you about the 333,488 obstacles that I overcame single-handedly. Number one, I...*

Instead, use a **PowerPhrase for Accepting Compliments From the Boss,** such as:

- **Thank you. That means a lot, especially from you.**

- **Thank you. It helped that I had such great support from my team.**
- **Thank you. I feel great about it too.**
- **Thank you for noticing.**

How do you respond to criticism from a supervisor? Do not say:

— *You're wrong.*

— *You don't have a clue what I do for you.*

— *After all that I do for you, all you notice are the mistakes.*

— *Whatever you say…*

— *Yeah, but YOU…*

Instead, respond with a **PowerPhrase for Accepting Criticism,** such as:

Even weaknesses can be turned in to strengths at performance reviews.

- **I wasn't aware that there was a problem. I want to hear your feedback to understand what needs to be changed.**
- **I understand how you might have viewed it that way. Next time, I will handle it by doing… I want to do whatever I can to strengthen our working relationship. I consider us a team.**[7]
- **I plan to take this information and devise a plan to improve my performance.**

One powerful way to respond to criticism is to seek clarification of the speaker's point of view.

- **What else would you like to see me do differently?**
- **What do you mean by…?**
- **Do I understand you correctly that…?**
- **What needs to be done at this point?**

A performance review is a good time to request the resources you need to do a better job. Don't say:

[7] *How to Prepare for Your Annual Performance Review* By Susan Fenner, Education & Professional Development Manager, IAAP World Headquarters

— *I can't meet my objectives because you...*

— *I am not getting the results I want because I do not have...*

Instead use a **PowerPhrase to Request Resources,** such as:

- **A few things that would increase my productivity are...**
- **My research has shown that these are the costs... and these are the savings... of obtaining the following resources...**

Breaking Bad New to the Boss

Do you ever have bad news to give the boss? Don't just say:

— *That idiot Jenkins withdrew his account. He just wasn't patient enough to see this thing through.*

— *I won't meet the deadline.*

— *I should have...*

A performance review is a good time to request the resources you need to do a better job.

Instead, do your homework before speaking. Make sure there really is a problem. Then do not delay. Come armed with all possible solutions. Look ahead to the future.

Use a **PowerPhrase for Breaking Bad News to the Boss,** such as:

- **I made a mistake. I did not realize...**(that Jenkins needed more consistent updates than most of our clients require, and I updated him as I do our other clients.) **He...**(became nervous and withdrew his account before our approach had a chance to pay off.) **Some measures I have taken are...**
- **I have some bad news. There have been...**(major delays) **and...**(we are unable to meet the quality requirements within the given deadline.) **Here are three recommendations of how we can address the**

client's concerns. Number 1….

- **To do the best job possible, I need one more week.**
- **Next time I will …**

If you want to introduce the subject in a humorously humble way, say:

- **I just made a career-limiting move.**

Admit mistakes and move on to giving your best.

When you break bad news to your boss, come armed with all possible solutions.

Power Pointer–Admit Fault When Appropriate

Lisa was contracted by a bank to be a mystery shopper to discover what services competing banks offer. Unfortunately, her report got forwarded to one of the bank representatives that she had been investigating. The representative sent a reply email asking what was going on and if Lisa was legitimately interested in her services. Lisa was embarrassed, and wondered how to respond.

I shared the following three-step process that research shows mends fences as quickly as possible. Say:

- **I'm sorry.**
- **Please forgive me.**
- **It will never happen again.**

If you really messed up, follow this with:

- **How can I make it up to you?**

Lisa made her call immediately. The representative completely understood and Lisa was very glad that she did not attempt to cover over the truth. Don't hide—admit the truth!

Power Tip Put Things in Context

In "How to Deal With Difficult People", Paul Freidman tells of an ad executive that mishandled an account. He began his report to the board of directors by placing a black dot on a white sheet. When asked what they saw, he said "a black dot." He replied:

- **Yes, and there is also a large white sheet of paper. Notice when something is blemished we attend to that blemish and overlook the broad background on which it is placed. I hope you keep that background in mind when I make my report this morning.**

While humbly admitting mistakes, sometimes we need to help them maintain perspective.

Speaking With the Boss's Authority

When you speak on your boss's behalf, be willing to remind people of whom you represent.

There are times when you will speak on the boss's behalf and need to speak with his or her authority. Be willing to remind people whom you represent. Don't say:

— *I was wondering if maybe you could…*

— *Here's what I want you to do…*

Instead, use a **PowerPhrase for Communicating With Your Boss's Authority,** such as:

- **Ms. Big has sent me to get the following files…**
- **I know Mr. Big's expectations. This is what must be done…**
- **Joe Important did not suggest that there would be any problem in obtaining your support on his behalf.**

These phrases carry more impact when the boss has credentialized you his or herself. Some supervisors use

PowerPhrases to Credentialize Their Staff, such as:

- **When ______ opens her mouth my voice comes out.**
- **While I am away I expect you to regard what ______ says as if you heard it from me.**
- **She's the boss when I'm gone.**

If you need to be credentialized, ask your supervisor to use one of these expressions.

It is in your interest as well as your boss's interest that you assertively ask for what you need in a straightforward assertive way. That is what your PowerPhrases at work are for.

If you need to be credentialized, ask your supervisor.

CHAPTER 9

PowerPhrases™ at Work: Communicating With Coworkers

Coworkers can be your allies… or your adversaries. Be sure to cultivate coworkers as allies at every level of the organization, from the janitor, to the mailroom, to the CEO.

Offer help and ask for help when you need it. For example, if you are making labels, ask yourself who else can use labels. Then offer:

- **Joan, I'm making labels, do you want some too?**

Ask:

- **What can I do for you?**

Say:

- **I need your help.**

These are all PowerPhrases.

Cultivate coworkers as allies at every level of the organization.

Take an interest in your peers. Listen, listen, and listen. It is amazing to hear people go on and on without realizing that they haven't asked about the other person. Often it is to your advantage to allow that. You can learn a lot just listening and encouraging them to speak. Don't say:

— *I'd like to get to know you. Let me tell you all about myself.*

— *Let me tell you about the week I had. It all started with…*

Instead use a **PowerPhrase for Expressing Interest,** such as:

- **There is so much I want to learn from you.**
- **Tell me what it's like for you around here.**
- **I'd like a chance to speak with you. When can we arrange that?**
- **Do you mind if I pick your brain?**
- **Can I take you to lunch?**

Be sure to solicit support for your ideas from your colleagues to encourage buy-in. Rather than simply asking for support, GIVE them something. Use a **PowerPhrase for Soliciting Support for an Idea,** such as:

- **Joan, I want to give you the first chance to review the XYZ proposal before the meeting. Your recommendations and support will help it in the approval process.**
- **I invite your involvement in the spring-loaded widget project in its early development when you can still help shape things. Your expertise can make a huge difference here.**

Rather than simply asking for support, GIVE coworkers something.

Giving Feedback to Coworkers

We all like to look good in front of our employers, so give positive feedback in front of others, and corrective feedback in private. Question the urge to give corrective feedback before you do it. When someone suggests an idea and requests your feedback, avoid being a wet blanket and saying things like:

— *What's wrong with the way things are now?*

— *You're kidding, right?*

If that is your first impulse, reply with a **PowerPhrase to Buy Time to Consider an Idea,** such as:

- **That's an interesting idea.**
- **I never thought of that.**

When you do give feedback, consider the following.

1. Feedback Needs to Be Specific.

They need to be able to apply the ideas. Don't say:

— *Great job!*

— *You could have done a better job.*

Instead use a **PowerPhrase for Specific Feedback,** such as:

- **I particularly like the way you did A. What I like most about how you did it is...**
- **A, B and C work well. Some suggestions I have for D, E and F are...**

2. Feedback Needs to Be Solution Oriented.

If there are problems, focus on how they can be fixed. Don't say:

— *This is wrong and that is wrong and everything else is awful too.*

Feedback needs to be solution oriented.

Instead use a **PowerPhrase for Offering Solutions in Feedback,** such as:

- **One way to strengthen A is... Have you considered ____ for B? C could be improved by...**

3. Feedback Needs to Express Facts as Facts and Opinions as Opinions.

Don't say:

— *The exercises were useless.*

Say:

- **I did not see the value in the exercises.**

4. Feedback Needs to Be Consistent.

If you wait to give feedback until there is a problem, people will resist. Be sure to tell people how much you appreciate everything they do even if they are just "doing their job." Use a **PowerPhrase for Consistent Feedback.**

- **I want to let you know how much I appreciate your ___ every day.**
- **Thanks for making my job easier by…**
- **I always appreciate the way you…**
- **Thank you for ___.**

Say it and walk away. If you glance back you will see their jaw drop open because chances are good they were expecting a "but" followed by everything they do wrong.

Be sure to consistently give positive feedback in addition to pointing out problem areas.

Power Pointer–Use the Power of Praise

When doing training for The Department of Defense, I had the group do an exercise that is recommended by Barbara Fielder in "Motivation in the Workplace". She gives everyone ten coins to put in their pocket. Then she has them circulate and acknowledge each other. Every time they acknowledge someone, they transfer a coin from one pocket to the other. The goal is to transfer all coins by the end of the day.

I gave this group five coins and three days to do the exercise in, but only a few did it. Finally I called an acknowledgement break. I told them they could not sit down until they had transferred all five coins. No one moved. It took several minutes of insisting until someone finally started the process.

The room transformed once the group finally got started. Hearts opened and people were delighted. Individuals who had been in conflict with each other acknowledged things they appreciated about each other.

Try the ten-coin exercise and see what it does for you.

Handling Interruptions

Do you hate it when people poke their heads in and say, "Got a minute?" What they are really asking is "Are you doing something that is more important than I am?" Ask yourself the same question.

To handle interruptions, use the three-step process for saying no. Begin with an acknowledgement of the request. Then briefly describe your situation. Finally, reaffirm the relationship.

Handling Interruptions Using the Three-Step Process for Saying No

Acknowledge	Circumstance	Transform
Yes, I see what you are asking.	I have a 2:00 deadline.	I can talk with you after that.
I'd like to help.	5 minutes is all I have.	Will that help?
This would require my full attention.	I don't have it to give right now.	I believe you can handle it yourself.
I understand what you need.	Now is not a good time.	If you still need help tomorrow I might be able to fit it in.

Speak up when someone expresses your idea and takes credit for it.

PowerPhrases for Meetings

You have a chance to shine at meetings, as well as a chance to practice all of your positive office politics skills. For example, what do you do when someone expresses your idea and takes credit for it? Speak up. Don't let it pass, and don't say:

— *Hey, that was my idea! You stole it!*

Instead, use a **PowerPhrase for Taking Credit for Your Ideas,** such as:

- **I believe that idea started with a comment I made earlier. I want to elaborate on my thinking.**

- **That is what I was referring to when I said… I am glad you like my idea, and I like the way you elaborated on it.**

Later you can address the offender using the conflict model from Chapter 4. I recommend that you also ask someone:

- **Is there something about the way I present my ideas that makes it hard to take them seriously?**

When you have the floor and someone interrupts, ask yourself if you are being wordy and trying his or her patience. If not, use a **PowerPhrase to Handle Interrupters,** such as:

- **Excuse me. I wasn't finished yet.**
- **I want to hear what you have to say as soon as I am done.**

When you have the floor and someone interrupts, use a PowerPhrase to handle interrupters.

If someone is dominating the discussion, say:

- **You have great ideas on the subject. Let's open the floor up for input from others.**
- **Since the agenda allows us only another ten minutes on this topic, we need to keep this moving. Please give us the condensed version and allow time for other comments before ending this discussion.**

Sometimes you can simply say:

- **There is only time for the short version, please.**

Encouraging Participation

If you are leading the meeting, one of your responsibilities is to encourage input from members who may not speak without encouragement. Simply say:

- **___, what is your opinion on the subject?**

If they do not offer an opinion, it is appropriate to ask again, by saying:

- **Your ideas do not need to be polished. We need to**

know what direction your thinking is taking.

When there is a side conversation going on, it needs to be addressed. **Use a PowerPhrase for Addressing a Side Conversation,** such as:

- **Please give Bill your full attention.**
- **When Bill finishes, I invite your comments.**
- **We all want to end this meeting on time, and that requires speaking one at a time.**
- **We have a lot of material to cover, and I'd rather not get off track. At the break let's get together, and this way I'll be able to give your concerns more individual attention.**

If someone is late, rather than reviewing what he or she missed, tell the offender:

- **Be sure to ask someone to catch you up on what was missed later.**

Address the issue of ongoing lateness later.

When issues are brought up that are not on the agenda, rather than addressing the inappropriate topic, use a **PowerPhrase for Maintaining the Agenda,** such as:

- **That's an important topic. Please make sure that it gets on the agenda for a future meeting.**

When there is a side conversation going on during a meeting, it needs to be addressed.

Handling Backstabbing Coworkers

If you hear about someone talking about you behind your back, make your **CASE. Clarify** what you have heard, and **assert** yourself using the steps outlined in chapter 3. You can then **seek** solutions and **evaluate** them.

Assert Yourself With Backstabbers

Problem	Impact: Thoughts/ Feelings/Effect	Request	Consequence
When I heard that you complained to others about the quality of my work…	I was devastated. I questioned our working relationship and began to wonder how safe it is to be open with you.	In the future, come to me directly if there is an issue.	I will do the same for you.
I confided in you, and I have reason to believe that you shared my secrets with others.	This can destroy our working relationship.	What can I do to ensure that my confidences are honored?	I will only confide in you if I feel secure.

Backstabbing is passive-aggressive, and needs to be addressed straightforwardly.

Backstabbing is passive-aggressive, and needs to be addressed straightforwardly. Use the four step process to assert yourself clearly.

Dealing With Unsolicited Advice

When a coworker gives you unsolicited advice, again, make your **CASE**. Be sure you clarify their intent before asserting yourself. Then use some or all of the four-step model to assert yourself, followed by seeking solutions and evaluating them.

Dealing With Unsolicited Advice

Problem	Impact: Thoughts/ Feelings/Effect	Solution/ Request	Consequence
When you offer advice,	I get confused.	Please refrain from advising me unless I request it.	I will do the same for you.
When you tell me how to do my job,	I think you do not trust me.		

Communicate clearly and effectively with your coworkers and enjoy the clarity that comes with PowerPhrases.

Enjoy the clarity that comes with PowerPhrases.

CHAPTER 10

PowerPhrases™ at Work: Magic Phrases for Managers

Your success as a manager or supervisor begins at the interview. Hiring the right people is one of the most important things you can do. Know what questions to ask. There are many standard interview questions that are effective.

- **Why do you want this job?**
- **What are your strengths?**
- **What are your weaknesses?**
- **What makes you the best candidate?**
- **Why should I hire you?**

Marlene Caroselli suggests a few more unusual questions.

- **Tell me about myself.** (Yes, you read it right. The purpose is to assess the candidate's judgment of character.)
- **If you were the president of this company, what is one new policy/plan/product you would initiate?**[8]

A good interview question addresses the job the applicant is applying for and how they would handle a specific situation.

A good interview question addresses the job the applicant is applying for and how they would handle a specific situation.

- **What would you do to increase consumer widget awareness?**

[8] Marlene Caroselli, *Hiring and Firing*, Mission, KS: SkillPath Publications 1993

- **When two managers insist that you give their projects priority, how do you handle it?**
- **What are you most proud about in your previous job?**
- **How do you solve problems?**
- **This job calls for... What is your experience in this?**
- **This job requires... Tell me about your success in this area.**
- **What would your previous staff/bosses say about you?**

Marlene Caroselli also recommends that you use open-ended questions that start with...

Use open-ended questions that draw the candidates out.

- **What...**
- **Explain...**
- **Describe...**
- **How would you...?**
- **In what ways...**
- **Under what circumstance do you...?**
- **If you could...**
- **Please cite some examples of...**
- **Tell me about...**[9]

Avoid asking questions that can get you in legal problems. Find safe ways to get the information you require.

Don't say:

— *What kind of accent do you have?*

Say:

- **Do you have legal verification of your right to work in this country?**

[9] Marlene Caroselli, *Hiring and Firing,* Mission KS: SkillPath Publications 1993

Don't say:

— *What's your native language?*

Say:

- **What languages do you speak, read or write?**

Don't say:

— *Are you religious?*

Say:

- **These are the hours, days and shifts that are to be worked. Is there anything that would interfere with your ability to work these hours?**

Don't say:

— *How old are you?*

Say:

- **If we hire you, do you have proof of your age?**

Avoid asking questions that can get you in legal problems.

Don't say:

— *Do you have kids?*

Say:

- **Are you comfortable with our policy of not allowing personal phone calls at work?**

Don't say:

— *Does your disability keep you from being able to…?*

Say:

- **Is there anything that keeps you from being able to…?**

Other questions include:

- **I see you worked at ___ from ___ to ___. Why did you choose that firm?**

Be aware that many applicants supply false information. Probe to discover what is valid.

When you turn down a potential applicant, be prepared to explain why.

Power Preparation

The PowerPhrases listed for interviews and terminations are not meant to replace legal advice. Be sure you clearly understand the laws of hiring and firing as well as your company's policies. Be certain that your words and actions conform to the Civil Rights Act of 1964, The American Disabilities Act of 1990 and the Equal Employment Opportunity Act of 1972.

End the interview by saying:

- **What happens next is…**
- **You can expect to hear back by…**

You probably do not enjoy turning down a potential applicant. When you do, be prepared to explain why. Be kind of course. The information may be helpful to them next time. If you can, say:

- **It was a tough decision.**
- **We found someone with a few skills and a different kind of training that we need.**

If there is something specific that disqualified them, let them know.

- **Next interview you have, I recommend that you…**
- **We felt you were under-prepared for the interview.**

Orienting New Employees

On the employee's first day, make a special effort to get them off to a great start. Don't greet new employees by saying:

— *Good luck!*

— *You're on your own.*

When orienting new employees, use positives to express

company policy. Don't say:

— *Don't steal.*

— *Don't come to work looking skuzzy.*

Instead use **PowerPhrases to Orient New Employees,** such as:

- **We expect our employees to safeguard company property from theft.**
- **We require our employees to dress according to the following dress code.**

Go on to orient new employees by saying:

- **The history, mission and goals of the department/company are…**
- **We are glad you are here!**
- **What questions do you have?**
- **Let me introduce you around. This is…**
- **Your job responsibilities are…**
- **When you get stuck, here's what you do.**
- **When you need help, this is whom you turn to.**

When giving employees assignments, whether they are new or old, be sure to follow the recommendations for delegation.

Delegation is a five-step process.

Delegation

Do you resist delegating or do it ineffectively? Delegation is a five-step process. Delegating consists of:

1. An optional opening,
2. A benefit to them,
3. A clear description of what is to be done,
4. A confirmation of understanding of the task, and
5. A confirmation of commitment.

There are PowerPhrases for each.

Make sure the person that you are delegating to knows what they can gain from taking the task on.

1. Opening

Do not open with:

— *You don't look busy. Will you…?*

— *I'm asking you to do this because I don't want to…*

— *I hate to ask you but…*

— *Sorry to bother you but…*

— *I was wondering if maybe you would…*

Instead use a **PowerPhrase Opener for Delegation,** such as:

- **Although I am aware of how busy you are, I have a request…**
- **I would never ask you to do something I would not do myself…**
- **There is an opportunity here for you to…**
- **I'm asking you because I know I can trust you…**

Then make sure they know what they can gain from taking the task on.

2. Benefit

Follow the request with a **PowerPhrase for Communicating a Benefit to Them**, such as:

- **What this means to you is…**
- **This will help you by…**
- **If you do this for me I will…**
- **I'll make sure my boss knows how you made a difference when I really needed you.**

3. Describe

Be sure the task description is clear. Don't say:

— *I need this sometime.*

— *Here. You figure it out.*

Instead, use a **PowerPhrase to Ensure a Clear Description,** such as:

- **I need ________ by ________ because________.**
- **Here is what needs to happen…**
- **I have written out instructions. Let's go over them together.**
- **The deadline is ___, the quality specifications are ___ and the budget is ___. Of these three, the priority in this project is ___.**

4. Confirm

Confirm their understanding of the task. Don't say:

— *Do you have any questions?*

— *Do you understand?*

Be sure the task description is clear.

Instead, ask open-ended questions, using a **PowerPhrase to Confirm Understanding,** such as:

- **What did I leave out?**
- **What would you like reviewed?**
- **What will your first step be?**
- **Let me make sure my instructions are clear. What is your understanding of what I have told you?**
- **What questions do you have?**
- **What ideas do you have about…?**
- **What do you think about…?**

5. Commitment

Be sure to have a firm commitment before leaving the task to them. Use a **PowerPhrase for Getting Commitment,** such as:

- **Can I count on you?**

- **When will you have that for me?**

Put it all together into:

The Five-Step Process for Delegating

Combine phrases from the different categories to make your request powerful without being overbearing.

Opening	What's in it for Them	Clear Request	Confirm Understanding	Get Commitment
I would never delegate anything I wasn't willing to do my self.[10]	What this means for you is____.	I need ___ by ___ because___.	What did I leave out?	When will you have that?
There is something important that needs to be done.	If you help us out here I will make sure my boss knows how you pitched in.	I have clear written instructions. I would like to go over them with you.	What can I clarify?	Can we count on you for this?
I need your help...	If you do this for me I will...	My situation is... and I need...	What questions can I answer for you?	Will you do this for me?

Get a firm commitment before leaving the task to them.

The Four-Step Process for Delegating

The first steps can be combined. You can open with a statement that offers a benefit.

[10] Mark Tower, *Dynamic Delegation*, Mission, KS: SkillPath Publications 1993

Opening — What's in it for them	Clear Request	Confirm Understanding	Get Commitment
This is a critical task that must be done. It is not just busy work.[11]	What I need is... The deadline is... The budget is...	Let me make sure my instructions were clear. What is your understanding of the task?	Let's schedule the first follow-up session.
I have an opportunity for you that will help you learn how to...	This is the objective..., this is the means..., these are the boundaries...	How will you begin?	When will you begin?

In *Dynamic Delegation*, Mark Tower observes: "The delegator must keep what he or she wants to give up-responsibility. Conversely, he or she must give up what he or she wants to keep–authority."[12] Be sure to give the authority to your delegatee and let others know that they have it. Some are listed in Chapter 8. Other **PowerPhrases to Credentialize Your Employees** are:

Give the authority to your delegate and let others know that they have it.

- **___ speaks for me.**
- **When ___ asks for something I expect you to give it to her.**
- **___ is in charge of ___. Please give her your full cooperation.**

Schedule follow-up sessions. At these sessions you can use a **PowerPhrase for Following-Up on Delegation,** such as:

- **Please give us an update of your progress.**
- **Is the project running on schedule?**
- **Is everything within budget?**
- **Are the quality specifications being met?**
- **What can I do to support your work?**

[11] Mark Tower, *Dynamic Delegation*, Mission KS: SkillPath Publications 1993
[12] Mark Tower, *Dynamic Delegation*, Mission KS: SkillPath Publications 1993

Of course you may not like the answers that you get. You might find that you need to coach.

Coaching Employees

Coaching through problems is a matter of making your CASE. (1) **Clarify** their position, (2) **Assert** yourself, (3) **Seek** solutions, (4) **Evaluate** options and create agreements.

1. Clarify Their Position

When you clarify their position, ask questions and LISTEN. Find things to acknowledge in their work.

When you clarify their position, ask questions and LISTEN.

Do not say:

— *I'll do the talking around here.*

— *Why should I listen to you?*

— *You idiot! You blew it again!*

Instead, use a **PowerPhrase to Solicit Their Perspective**, such as:

- **What do you think of your performance?**
- **Do you understand why there is a problem with your behavior?**
- **How do you see the problem?**

Listen carefully and acknowledge what they say before explaining your perspective.

2. Assert Your Position

Do not limit your comments to where they fall short of expectations. Instead, begin with mention of whatever positives you can comfortably acknowledge. Use a **PowerPhrase for Acknowledging Their Work**, such as:

- **I like the way you did…**
- **This work shows a lot of attention to detail…**
- **I see progress with…**

- **Your... in the face of... means a lot.**[13]

Follow with a description of the problem. Again, be specific and unless it is obvious, describe why it is a problem. Don't say:

— *You could have done a better job.*

— *It's not good enough.*

— *This is terrible.*

Instead, use a **PowerPhrase for Describing the Problem,** such as:

- **The problem with _____ is that ____, which results in ___. (The problem with this report is that it lacks detail, which leaves questions in the reader's mind.)**
- **What doesn't work so well is ___ because ___. (What doesn't work is the summary because new information is introduced which causes confusion.)**
- **I see a problem with ____ that could cause ____.**

The best solutions are the ones employees come up with on their own or that you come up with together.

3. Seek Solutions

Put most of your effort into discussing solutions. Talk about what you want more than what you don't want. If you want to encourage them to solve more of their own problems, avoid dictating solutions. Encourage them to develop a habit of thinking for themselves. The best solutions are the ones they come up with on their own–or that you come up with together.

Don't say:

— *Do it this way.*

— *I don't know what to do—you figure it out.*

— *Any idiot knows that the best way to do it is...*

Instead, use a **PowerPhrase for Creating Solutions,** such as:

[13] Donald Weiss, *Why Didn't I Say That?* New York: Amacom Publications, 1994

- **Let's look at what works and figure out what we can learn to deal with the problems.**
- **My recommendation is... What do you think?**
- **How do you plan to proceed?**
- **What do you intend to do about the problem?**
- **Let's look for solutions together.**
- **Here is another way of doing it.**
- **What do you suggest that we do to keep this from happening again?**
- **What is your plan to upgrade quality?**
- **What would it take to ___ (ex. get you on time with deadlines)?**

4. Evaluate Options and Create Agreements

Solutions need to be realistic in order to be effective.

Your solutions need to be realistic in order to be effective. If someone has a swearing problem, a zero-tolerance policy is unlikely to work. They might mean well, but the first time they drop something on their toe, watch them let it fly! Use a **PowerPhrase to Evaluate Options,** such as:

- **Does this option solve the problem?**
- **Do you believe that you can comply with this option?**
- **Is there any way this option can be improved?**
- **Is this an option that you will be able to commit to in writing?**

Be sure to get the commitment in writing, and arrange for your follow up meeting.

You can use this structure for coaching in performance reviews as well.

The Performance Review

Begin the review by making the employee as comfortable as you can. Start with a welcome and an overview of the procedure.

- **As you know, this is an opportunity for us to share information about your job, to clarify objectives and to see to how things are going for you.**
- **Then we can discuss growth.**
- **I will put my calls on hold so we won't be interrupted.**

Then go directly into reviewing goals and reviewing performance.

- **Let us compare notes on your top three goals and means to achieve them.**
- **Please give me examples.**
- **What will it take for you to meet your next quarter's goals?**

Where performance needs to be improved, refer back to the section about coaching employees as well as the following phrases.

Begin a performance review by making the employee as comfortable as you can; then go directly into reviewing goals and reviewing performance.

When you must refuse a request from an employee, ACT.

PowerPhrases for Improving Performance

Acknowledge	Describe Problem	Find Solutions
I like the way you ___.	What does not work as well is ___ because___ results in ___.	Let's look for solutions together.
I see progress with ___.	What I see that still needs work is...	How do you plan to proceed?
This work shows a lot of attention to detail.	Until the last page.	How can you add detail to the last page?
Generally I am very pleased with your work.	One area needs work. Perhaps I haven't made it clear that you are responsible for... and some problems are...	How can I help you succeed?
While I have seen improvement in quality,	when you...(submit the work for a big project three days late), the effect is...(we all have to wait before revisions can be made). We feel... (frustrated and angry).	Let's talk about time management.
I see progress with ___.	What I see that still needs work is...	How do you plan to proceed?

PowerPhrases for Refusing Requests From Employees

When you must refuse a request from an employee, use the ACT formula for saying no from Chapter 3. Acknowledge the request, briefly explain circumstances of why you are unable to grant it, and transform the refusal into a positive.

Acknowledge	Circumstances	Transform
I understand you are asking for...	I am unable to fulfill your request because...	What I can do is...
I am delighted with the work you have been doing the few months you have been here.	You haven't been here very long and the policy does not allow me to even consider a raise before the first year.	Let's review your performance and set goals so that when the first year mark comes, you will get the largest increase possible.
I appreciate your need for more money.	At present your performance does not merit consideration for a raise.	Let's review the two areas where improvement would indicate a raise in the future.
We love having you here.	We simply cannot afford a raise at this time.	You have a great future here and I hope you will stay until things turn around in this company.
I am aware that the computer that is assigned to you is slow.	Based on the amount of computer work you do, I cannot justify the expense of a new one.	If you can show me something I am overlooking I am happy to reconsider.
I agree that improvements in the warehouse are needed.	Funding only allows for a few.	Let's get some representatives to make suggestions on which ones they will be.

When an employee must be discharged for non-performance reasons, the words are never easy to find.

Termination

When the appropriate coaching sessions fail to bring positive results and standards have not been met, or when an employee must be discharged for non-performance related reasons, the words are never easy to find.

Power Questions to Ask Yourself Prior to Termination

In Hiring and Firing by Marlene Caroselli, E.D., Marlene quotes Stephen M. Karas, First Vice President, Manager of Major Buildings Division for Security Pacific Bank as saying that prior to terminating anyone, he asks himself the following questions:

- **Did I do everything I could to assist this person?**
- **Did I communicate properly?**
- **Did he or she have all the tools necessary to do the job?**

It is tempting to assume that the employee who did not work out is the problem. Powerful managers look to themselves to see what is to be learned from the experience.

Before termination the employee usually already suspects the inevitable.

Usually the employee already suspects the inevitable. Your job is to make it as quick and clean as possible, and to preserve as much of the other person's dignity as you can. Begin with an opening, explain the situation in a minimum of detail, and reaffirm the other person.

Use statements that encourage the terminated employee toward action.

The Three-Step Process for Termination

Opening	Explain	Reaffirm
I suspect you have guessed what this meeting is about.	In our prior meetings we have outlined the standards you must meet to stay on with us and they have not been met.	HR has a few leads for other jobs.
I am forced to terminate your employment.	Despite warnings your performance level has not reached acceptable levels.	I hope you find work that suits you in the future.
I feel sad to tell you,	budget cutbacks have forced the elimination of your position.	I understand that Extraordinary Widgets is looking for people with your qualifications.
I have bad news for you.	Your employment here is terminated.	How can I help you pull resources together?
We have come to a final decision regarding your employment.	The reasons are as follows…	Personnel will discuss your final pay and collect your office keys.
I have to terminate your employment effective immediately.	You have been told what to expect and been given written warnings, but the expectations have not been met.	I wish this could have been resolved otherwise.

Make termination as quick and clean as possible, and to preserve the other person's dignity.

Power Thinking–Effective Management Requires Powerful Decision Making

It might comfort you to know that while immediately following a firing, 75% described the firing as the "worst thing that ever happened to them"; one year later the vast majority describes it as "the best thing that ever happened."[14] Of course, as a supervisor, your first loyalty is to the organization. Many times that requires you to be firm.

Termination is probably the most difficult part of managing. As with any other aspect of management, it requires assertively saying what you mean, meaning what you say without being mean when you say it.

Good management requires good PowerPhrases.

Good management requires good PowerPhrases. From the initial interview and throughout your role as manager, use PowerPhrases to make yourself more effective. In the next chapter you will learn how to create your own.

[14] Marlene Caroselli, Hiring and Firing, Mission, KS: SkillPath Publications 1993

CHAPTER 11

Now It's Your Turn—Create Your Own PowerPhrases™

What would life be like if you could say what you wanted whenever you wanted? Can you imagine the freedom of always being able to say what you mean, and not have to worry about anyone ever taking offense? Wouldn't it be great if the honest expression of whatever you thought and felt always got good results?

In my fantasy world the raw truth works every time, but in the real world, it is in your best interests to edit. You discovered the need to edit early in life. Speaking your mind would backfire! Unfortunately you probably took self-editing too far. You probably did not just edit your words. My guess is that you also edited what you were willing to become conscious of thinking and feeling.

What would life be like if you could say what you wanted whenever you wanted?

Read that paragraph again, because it is huge in its implications for PowerPhrases. It is also huge in implications for your life.

To create your own effective PowerPhrases you first must become aware of what it is that you would say in the perfect world I described above. Then edit your words to get the results you desire.

You have been editing your thoughts and feeling for so long, that it will take work to uncover the truth now. An excellent way is through writing.

What would you really like to say to your boss if you

knew there would be no negative repercussions? Would you ever say something like this?

— *Listen, you narcissist—this conversation is getting us nowhere. They might pay you three times what they pay me to bore the people that work for you with your empty accomplishments, but I happen to take my job seriously and I have more important things to do than to hear you brag about nothing. You are so pitiful, and if I didn't feel like puking I might feel sorry for you.*

Does it feel good to express it to paper? (Do be careful about what you do with that paper.) After getting clarity about your thoughts, feelings and what you would LIKE to say in a situation like this, you will find it easier to say:

- **I prefer that we stay on the subject of our product line. Like you, I have a number of deadlines to meet.**

What would you really like to say if you knew there would be no negative repercussions?

Power Pointer–Finding Your Inner Voice Can Take Time

A song I wrote has the following lyrics:

So much of who I am is an illusion.

An act of who I think I'm spozed to be.

All this make-believe creates confusion.

I don't know what's real inside of me.

One of the hardest parts of PowerPhrases can be quieting your inner-editor long enough to learn what you would really like to say.

Eight Steps to Your Own PowerPhrases

Create Your Own PowerPhrases Using the Following Eight Steps:

1. Write a freeform letter saying what you would if my perfect world of free expression was a real one.
2. Review the letter for the essential message.
3. Determine what results you seek by communicating.
4. Start writing what you want to actually say, considering the results you want.
5. Ask yourself the PowerPhrase questions from the end of chapter 1. (See the review later in this chapter.)
6. Edit for killer phrases from chapter 2.
7. Run it by a friend.
8. Take a deep breath, use your pass the butter voice (described in the introduction) and express yourself.

The truth in your heart is multi-dimensional. Allow your inner truths to emerge.

Step One: Tools for Your Freeform Letter

Writing your freeform letter is a simple process; however, it is not an easy process. You will think it takes an eternity to discover what you really want to say. Some of your thoughts will contradict others. The truth in your heart is multi-dimensional. What makes sense at one level does not make sense at another. Do not be in too big of a hurry to make it all add up. Take your time. Allow your inner truths to emerge.

Ask yourself the following questions:

1. What might I be angry about?
2. What hurts?
3. What am I afraid of?
4. What do I regret?
5. Is there something I feel shame about that I do

not want to admit to myself or the other person?
6. What do I want to have happen?
7. What do I want this person to know?

Do not lie to yourself. This is simply information to be considered in discovering what it is you need and want, as well as in understanding how to get it. Now move to step 2.

Step 2: Review the Letter for the Essential Message

Once you have expressed yourself to paper, notice themes in your thoughts and feelings. Some of the things you write will seem insignificant. Others words will have a clear ring of truth. Note what ideas repeat. Notice what touches you the most emotionally when you review it. Also notice if you feel resistant to some of what you write. If you feel resistance to your words, ask yourself why. Is there something that you do not want to admit to yourself? Is there something that you do not want to have to tell someone else? Don't worry–you do not have to act on or express everything you think and feel–in fact I recommend that you don't! Do examine your responses to what you wrote to understand yourself better.

If you feel resistance to your words, ask yourself why.

Step 3: Determine What Results You Would Seek if You Did Communicate.

The power of a communication is best measured by the result it obtains. Be clear of your intention before you begin to formulate your PowerPhrases. Ask yourself:

1. Are you speaking to unburden yourself?
2. Are you speaking to get the other person to stop doing something?
3. Are you speaking to get the other person to start doing something?
4. Are you speaking to create a bond?
5. Are you speaking to relay information?

6. Are you speaking to punish or extract revenge? (Not recommended.)

The words you choose will depend on the result you want to accomplish.

Step 4: Start Writing What You Want to Actually Say, Keeping the Results in Mind.

Refer back to your intention and your freeform writing as you begin to formulate your own PowerPhrases. Also refer to the chapters that relate most to your issue. If you need to say no, refer to the **ACT** formula. If the issue is a conflict, make your **CASE**. Refer to the PowerPhrases I recommend, and create your own.

Step 5: Ask Yourself the PowerPhrase Questions From the End of Chapter One

Apply the PowerPhrase questions at the end of Chapter One to your writing. They are summarized below.

A. Is it short? Eliminate all unnecessary words.

B. Is it colorful? Can you find more powerful words?

C. Although you are editing your raw thoughts, does it say what you truly mean?

D. Are you certain that you are ready to back up your words with action?

E. Are there trigger words, accusations, and remarks that do not consider the self-esteem of your listener?

Apply the PowerPhrase questions from the end of Chapter One to your writing.

Step 6: Edit for Killer Phrases

Review your words one more time to make certain that there are no killer phrases listed in Chapter 2.

Step 7: Run it by a Friend

You are probably too involved with your own situation to be objective. Try your communication out on a friend. Ask your friend how he or she would respond if they received a communication like the one you prepared.

Step 8: Take a Deep Breath, Use Your Pass the Butter Voice and Express Yourself.

You can do it! Say what you mean, mean what you say, and do not be mean when you say it.

Be aware that if you are speaking more powerfully than usual, your listener will not necessarily appreciate it. If someone is used to being able to get whatever he or she wants from you, they may not be pleased when you express yourself strongly. Even if people are accustomed to an aggressive behavior from you, they may resist calm assertiveness. You need to mean what you say and believe in yourself as you follow up on your communication.

If you are speaking more powerfully than usual, your listener will not necessarily appreciate it.

PowerPhrases of Appreciation

PowerPhrases are not only for telling people what they need to change or what is not working. PowerPhrases are important to express the positives as well. When you review your freeform writing, pick out the words of appreciation that you find and be sure to express them as well. Below are a few of mine:

- **Bob, with all the people in the world that you could be spending your life with, thank you for choosing me.**
- **David, you are the best thing that ever happened to me.**
- **Harriet, I am so glad that my Dad found you.**
- **Cindi, your zest for life increases mine.**
- **Bill, your unconditional friendship gives me a much needed refuge.**
- **Andy, thanks for your acceptance of me wherever I am at any time.**

Now that you have the steps, start expressing yourself in such a way that others find out who you really are. Uncover your voice within and use PowerPhrases that allow that inner voice to be heard and understood.

PowerPhrases are not only for telling people what they need to change or what is not working. PowerPhrases are important to express the positives as well.

Chapter 12:

Silence is the Greatest PowerPhrase™ of All.

"The purpose of words is to create silence."

— *Pundit Ravi Shankar*

Why do we speak at all? The above quote suggests that we speak in order to create silence.

Some words create agitation. Some words result in questions. Some words result in confusion. True PowerPhrases result in silence.

True PowerPhrases produce peace. True PowerPhrases resolve questions. True PowerPhrases clear up confusion.

Remember from the introduction:

- **Less is more.**

Silence is the ultimate PowerPhrase.

Powerful communicators know when to speak and when to be quiet. Powerful communicators are not afraid of silence. Silence is the ultimate PowerPhrase.

BIBLIOGRAPHY

Books

Baber, Anne and Lynne Waymon. *Great Connections. Small Talk and Networking for Businesspeople.* Woodbridge, VA: Impact Publications. 1991.

Booher, Dianna. *The New Secretary.* New York: Facts on File Publications, 1985.

Booher, Dianna. *Communicate With Confidence.* New York: McGraw Hill. 1994.

Breitman, Patti, and Connie Hatch. *How to Say No Without Feeling Guilty.* New York: Bantam. 2000.

Caroselli, Marlene Ed.D. *Hiring & Firing.* Mission, KS: SkillPath Publications, 1991.

Caroselli, Marlene Ed.D. *Meetings that Work.* Mission, KS: SkillPath Publications, 1991.

Cohen, Herb. *You Can Negotiate Anything.* Don Mills Ontario: Lyle Stuart Inc, 1980.

Dobson, Michael and Deborah Singer. *Managing Up.* New York: Amacom, 1999.

Donaldson, Michael, and Mimi. *Negotiating for Dummies.* Foster City CA: IDG Books Worldwide, Inc., 1996.

Gamble, Michael & Teri. *Sales Scripts That Sell.* New York: Prentice Hall Publications, 1992.

Griffin, Jack. *How to Say It™ at Work.* Paramus N.J.: Prentice Hall Press, 1998.

Friedman, Paul. How to *Deal With Difficult People.* Mission, KS: SkillPath Publications, 1994.

Larsen, Linda. *True Power.* Sarasota, Florida: Brandywine Publications, 2000.

Levinson, Jay Conrad. *Guerrilla Negotiating.* New York: John Wiley & Sons, 1999.

Mindel, Phyllis. *How to Say It℠ for Women.* Paramus, N.J.: Prentice Hall Press, 2001.

Nickerson, Pat. *Managing Multiple Bosses.* New York: Amacom, 1999.

Pollan, M. Stephen and Mark Levine. *Lifescripts.* New York: Macmillan, 1996.

Rackman, Neil. *Spin Selling,* New York: McGraw Hill, 1988.

Schiffman, Stephan. *Cold Calling Techniques (That Really Work!).* Holbrook, MA.: Adams Media Corporation,1990.

Shouse, Deborah. *Breaking the Ice: How to Improve Your On-the-Spot Communications Skills.* Mission, KS.:SkillPath Publications, 1993.

Towers, Mark. *Dynamic Delegation,* Mission, KS: SkillPath Publications, 1993.

Weiss, Donald. *Why Didn't I Say That??* New York: Amacom, 1994.

Videos

Scofield, Carol. *Conflict Management Skills for Women.* Mission, KS: SkillPath Publications, 1994.

Audios

Covey, Stephen. *The 7 Habits of Highly Effective People.* Provo, Utah: Franklin Covey Co., 1889,1997.

Fine, Debra. *The Fine Art of Small Talk.* Boulder, CO.: Career Track, 1996.

Flemming, Dr. Carol. *The Serious Business of Small Talk.* Mission, KS: SkillPath Publications, 1996.

Larsen, Linda. *12 Secrets to High Self-Esteem.* Mission, KS: SkillPath Publications. 1999.

Speaker's Roundtable. The Pros Speak About Success. Mission, KS: SkillPath Publications, 1999.

Walther, George. *Power Talking Skills.* Boulder, CO.: Career Track™, 1991.

Meryl Runion, MSCI

The Truth About... Meryl Runion

Meryl Runion, MSCI
Power Potentials
www.powerpotentials.com
Keynotes, Training, Consulting
powerphrases@att.net

"Most people do not know what TRUE power is."

The Truth About... Meryl Runion

- **International Speaker.**
- **Published Author.**
- **Real World Trainer.**
- **Power Motivator.**
- **Vanderbilt Graduate.**
- **Certified Educational Therapist.**

Meryl Runion has:

- **A Masters Degree, Science of Creative Intelligence.**
- **Taught over 400 seminars for SkillPath Seminars**

Meryl Runion, MSCI, has been helping people and organizations reach their goals since 1974 as a speaker, trainer, health professional and consultant.

Meryl is available for keynotes, training and private consultations. Let Meryl Runion help your organization survive and thrive in today's world.

Specialties Include:

Power Communication

Power Organization & Productivity

Power Conflict Resolution

Power Relating

Power Leadership

Stress Management

Self Esteem

Any area where you or your organization can use more power is an area where you or your organization can use Meryl Runion.

Most Requested Programs Include:

PowerPhrases™: Communication Skills to Survive and Thrive in Today's Workplace. This program provides you with a unique collection of stock PowerPhrases to empower you in life's challenging situations. You will learn phrases to clear up conflict, to establish a connection, to move a negotiation to a more powerful outcome, and more.

Power Resolution: Conflict Survival School.

Conflict management skills are vital for healthy relationships. Conflict is inevitable! Meryl teaches the skills to walk calmly into conflict and straight through to resolution.

Office Manager, Assistant, Secretary and Miracle Worker: the Power Assistant. The level of responsibility that comes with support positions is higher than ever before. This seminar teaches how to master the new level of responsibility, and stay composed in the process.

Managing Up. Stay in sync with the person who signs your paycheck. Learn about office politics, power communications and when and how to be assertive with those you work for.

The Truth About Love. Learn about the three stages of intimate relationships and how to have stability and excitement at the same time.

Clients Include:

- Department of Defense
- Army Intelligence
- Gladstone Industries
- SkillPath Seminars
- Veteran's Administration
- Overhead Door
- Vermont Social and Rehabilitation Services
- KPMG Manhattan
- MDC Holdings
- Current USA Inc
- E-Steel
- Mount Holyoke College
- Hydromat Inc.
- Canastota Central Schools
- IBM Canada
- Indian Health Specialist
- S&K Holding Company
- Kristi Lin's Academy
- World Plan Executive Council
- Sieman Corporation
- Sugen Corp
- Traveler's Insurance
- Colorado Energy Management
- The Patent Office of the United Kingdom; (Cardiff, Wales)
- Bevan and Ashford Solicitors; (Bristol, England)

Glowing Reports Include:

"Meryl Runion has a style that is both enthusiastic and caring. I loved the personal stories that she shared. Not only did the stories clarify the points she was making, they reminded me that we are all human. At times I laughed; at other times I was deeply touched. Meryl's presentation made the day fly. We sent 150 supervisors, managers, directors, and vice presidents as well those with leadership potential through her Conflict Resolution class. 100% of the evaluations were positive. Many thanked her for the learning. This learning was evident in the weeks that followed."

— *Dawn Roth, Director of the Call Center, Current Inc.*

"Meryl Runion is the best presenter I have ever seen or heard. I was impressed with her knowledge of the topic, the way she handled questions with ease, like there was nothing she couldn't handle. It definitely inspired me. Thanks!"

— *Julies Feagler, Administrative Assistant, Rhythms Net Communications*

"Meryl brought out the goodness in people that some thought they had lost. People feel better about working with each other."

— *Ida Hofner, Defense Depot, Department of Defense*

"I am a trainer for Current Inc., and I was thoroughly impressed with Meryl Runion's presentation. Her skills were unparalleled by any of my previous experiences. Thank you."

— *Chuck Anderson, Trainer, Current Inc*

"I was one of the fortunate women who attended the Women's Conference yesterday at the Double Tree Inn in Sea Tac, Washington. I especially want to thank Meryl for her dynamic presentations. I was so pumped up after my first session with her; I stayed with her for all of her remaining sessions. She is an inspiration and so gifted!"

— *Marilyn Bently, Senior Land Use Specialist, Whatcom County Planning and Development*

Meryl Runion, Power Potentials, power phrases@att.net

More Resources by Meryl Runion

PowerPhrases™! The Perfect Words to Say it Right and Get the Results You Want
Additional copies *$21.95*

Other Available Materials

Audiotapes:

Power Resolution: Conflict Management School

Learn the fundamentals of managing conflict. Discover the number one cause of conflict. Learn the tools to stay calm in conflict and the PowerPhrases to turn conflict into understanding. *Two Cassettes $21.95*

PowerPhrases™ That Work Audio

In this two-cassette tape you will not only learn PowerPhrases, but you will have the opportunity to hear how the PowerPhrases are expressed. Understand the fundamentals of PowerPhrases and learn many new PowerPhrases that have not been published elsewhere. *Two Cassettes $21.95*

The 10 Secrets of Genuine Power

Few people understand what genuine power is. Meryl Runion of Power Potentials has made a study of power, and will share her surprising discoveries in the "10 Secrets of Genuine Power." The first step in obtaining true power is in understanding what it is. Meryl provides this understanding, and then offers real-world concrete steps to obtaining and living genuine power in all aspects of life. *Two Cassettes $21.95*

The Truth About Love

This musical comedy tells a story about bad love gone good, and good love gone great. This cassette is clever, humorous and deeply insightful into the nature of codependency and love. Find out why author John Gray said —"I found the Truth About Love to be delightful, entertaining and informative." This cassette is rated "PG 13". *Single Cassette $12.95*

The Order Form

Item	Quantity		Price	Total
The Book:				
Additional copies of *PowerPhrases™! The Perfect Words to Say it Right and Get the Results You Want*	______	x	$21.95	______.__
Audiotapes:				
"Power Resolution: Conflict Management School", two cassettes	______	x	$21.95	______.__
"The 10 Secrets of Genuine Power", two cassettes	______	x	$21.95	______.__
"The Truth About Love", single cassette	______	x	$12.95	______.__
"PowerPhrases™! That Work", two cassettes	______	x	$21.95	______.__
Add $3.75 shipping for your first item	______	x		$3.75
$1.75 for each additional item.	______	x	$1.75	______.__
	TOTAL			______.__

Send to:

Power Potentials Publishing
PO Box 184
Cascade CO 80809

powerphrases@att.net

Or Order Online: www.powerpotentials.com

Send Your PowerPhrases to:

The PowerPhrase Clearinghouse

What are YOUR favorite PowerPhrases? Send them to the PowerPhrase Clearinghouse with written permission to use them. The most powerful will be published on the Power Potentials Website and in future PowerPhrase books.

What situations do you need a PowerPhrase for?

Email your challenging situations to the PowerPhrase Clearinghouse and we will either respond with a PowerPhrase for you or post your query for suggestions from others.

Sign up today for:
A Power Phrase a Week

A FREE weekly email newsletter

Send an email to *powerphrases@att.net* with subscribe in the subject line.

Privacy of all email addresses is respected.

You may unsubscribe at any time.

www.powerpotentials.com